Festivals of Attica

PUBLICATION OF THIS VOLUME HAS BEEN MADE POSSIBLE IN LARGE PART THROUGH THE GENEROUS SUPPORT AND ENDURING VISION OF WARREN G. MOON.

Festivals of Attica

An Archaeological Commentary

Erika Simon

The University of Wisconsin Press

The University of Wisconsin Press
1930 Monroe Street
Madison, Wisconsin 53711

www.wisc.edu/wisconsinpress/

3 Henrietta Street
London WC2E 8LU, England

5   4   3   2

Printed in the United States of America

Library of Congress Cataloging-in-Publication Data
Simon, Erika.
   Festivals of Attica.
   (Wisconsin studies in classics.)
   Includes bibliographical references and index.
   ISBN 0-299-09184-8 (pbk.: alk. paper)
   ISBN 0-299-09180-5 (pbk.: alk. cloth)
   1. Festivals—Greece. 2. Athens—Festivals, etc.
3. Gods, Greek. 4. Greece—Religious life and customs.
I. Title. II. Series.
DF123.S55   1982
394.2'6892'09385   81-70160

To Homer and Dorothy Thompson

CONTENTS

PLATES

Following page 54

Plate 1
　1 and 2. Calendar-frieze.
Plate 2
　1–3. Calendar-frieze. Elaphebolion to Boedromion.
Plate 3
　1–3. Calendar-frieze. Pyanopsion to Gamelion.
Plate 4
　1 and 2. Calyx-krater. Athenian months.
Plate 5
　1. Panathenaic amphora. Personification of the Olympiad.
　2. Oinochoe (chous). Dionysos and Pompe.
Plate 6
　1–3. Oinochoe. Dipolieia.
Plate 7
　1. Cup. Bouzyges plowing.
　2. Bell-krater. Bouzyges plowing.
Plate 8
　1. Bell-krater. Eleusinian scene.
　2. "Eleusinian pelike."
Plate 9
　Hydria. Eleusinian goddesses.
Plate 10
　1. "Regina Vasorum." Eleusinian scene.
　2. East pediment of the Parthenon. Eleusinian goddesses.
Plate 11
　Pinax of Niinnion.
Plate 12
　1. Fragment of an amphora of special shape. Procession for Athena Ergane.
　2. Apulian calyx-krater. Athena and the daughters of Kekrops.

ix

FIGURES

PREFACE

The six chapters of this book were Mary Flexner lectures given at Bryn Mawr College in the fall of 1978. I shall always remember with pleasure the months I spent in the beautiful setting of this distinguished place. My thanks go to the president, Mary Patterson McPherson, to the dean of the graduate school, Phyllis P. Bober, and to the colleagues who did me the honor of appointing me Flexner lecturer. I am most deeply indebted to Machteld J. Mellink and Brunilde S. Ridgway for their kindness and hospitality which I enjoyed from the very first day. Together with the other members of the department they gave me the feeling of belonging to the faculty, and the lectures profited greatly from their stimulating suggestions. My thanks go also to C. Stephen Jaeger and Kathleen W. Slane who spent much time in correcting my English text. Many good discussions with Richard and Maria Ellis, with James Wright and Kathleen Slane helped to shape these lectures. The same may be said of the eager students in my seminar on the Athenian gods and festivals; I remember with joy their reports and their interested questions. The manuscript of this book was completed in the spring of 1979. Publications after that date could not be taken into account. I wish to thank Pericles Georges of The University of Wisconsin Press for his editorial assistance.

For the illustrations of this book I am indebted to the museums and collections which are named in the captions of the plates. Furthermore I should like to thank C. Bérard (Lausanne), A. Birchall (London), B. Borell-Seidel (Hamburg), D. von Bothmer (New York), H. A. Cahn (Basel), J. Frel (Malibu), H. Froning (Würzburg), M. Hirmer (Munich), M. Maass (Munich), C. Melldahl (Göteborg), D. G. Mitten (Harvard University), M. Stettler (Steffisburg), and D. Thimme (Carlsruhe).

Much of my knowledge of ancient Athens I owe to Homer and Dorothy Thompson. To them this book is gratefully dedicated.

ABBREVIATIONS

I follow the list of abbreviations published in *AJA* 82 (1978) 5–10; *AJA* 84 (1980) 3–4. Other abbreviations used here are:

Aristotle, *AP*   Aristoteles, *Athenaion Politeia* ("The Constitution of the Athenians"), trans. J. Warrington (Everyman's Library: London and New York, 1976).

Bianchi   U. Bianchi, *The Greek Mysteries.* Iconography of Religions XVII, 3 (Leiden, 1976).

Bömer, "Pompa"   F. Bömer, s.v. "Pompa," *RE* 21.2 (1952) 1878–1974.

Brommer, *PF*   F. Brommer, *Der Parthenonfries* (Mainz, 1977).

Burkert, "Apellai"   W. Burkert, "Apellai und Apollon," *RhM* 118 (1975) 1–21.

Burkert, *HN*   W. Burkert, *Homo Necans.* Religionsgeschichtliche Versuche und Vorarbeiten 32 (Berlin, 1972).

Davies, *APF*   J. K. Davies, *Athenian Propertied Families 600–300 B.C.* (Oxford, 1971).

Deubner   L. Deubner, *Attische Feste* (Berlin, 1932).

Docs²   J. Chadwick, *Documents in Mycenaean Greek* (2nd edition: Cambridge, 1973).

"EleusD"   E. Simon, "Neue Deutung zweier eleusin-
                            ischer Denkmäler des 4. Jh. v. Chr.," *AntK* 9
                            (1966) 72–92.

Farnell   L. R. Farnell, *The Cults of the Greek States*
                            1–5 (Oxford, 1896–1909).

Ferguson   W. S. Ferguson, "The Salaminioi of Hepta-
                            phylai and Sounion," *Hesperia* 7 (1938) 1–74.

Froning   H. Froning, *Dithyrambos und Vasenmalerei
                            in Athen* (Würzburg, 1971).

Graf, *Eleusis*   F. Graf, *Eleusis und die orphische Dichtung
                            Athens in vorhellenistischer Zeit*. Religions-
                            geschichtliche Versuche und Vorarbeiten 33
                            (Berlin, 1974).

Hadzisteliou Price   Th. Hadzisteliou Price, *Kourotrophos* (Lei-
                            den, 1978).

Judeich   W. Judeich, *Topographie von Athen* (Munich,
                            1931).

Kahil, "ArtémisAtt"   L. Kahil, "Autour de l'Artémis attique," *AntK*
                            8 (1965) 20–33.

Kahil, "Brauron"   L. Kahil, "L'Artémis de Brauron: rites et
                            mystère," *AntK* 20 (1977) 86–98.

Kron   U. Kron, *Die zehn attischen Phylenheroen*,
                            AthMitt-BH 5 (Berlin, 1976).

Maass, *Prohedrie*   M. Maass, *Die Prohedrie des Dionysosthea-
                            ters in Athen*. Vestigia, Beiträge zur Alten
                            Geschichte 15 (Munich, 1972).

Melldahl/Flemberg   C. Melldahl and J. Flemberg, "Eine Hydria
                            des Theseus-Malers mit einer Opferdarstel-
                            lung," *From the Gustavianum Collections in
                            Uppsala* 2 (*Acta Universitatis Upsaliensis, Bo-
                            reas* 9: Uppsala 1978) 57–79.

Metzger	H. Metzger, *Recherches sur l'imagerie Athénienne* (Paris, 1965).
Meuli, *GesSch*	K. Meuli, *Gesammelte Schriften*, ed. Th. Gelzer (Basel and Stuttgart, 1975).
"Monatsbilder"	E. Simon, "Attische Monatsbilder," *JdI* 80 (1965) 105–123.
Mylonas	G. E. Mylonas, *Eleusis and the Eleusinian Mysteries* (Princeton, 1961).
Nilsson, *GF*	M. P. Nilsson, *Griechische Feste* (Leipzig, 1906).
Nilsson, *GGR*	M. P. Nilsson, *Geschichte der griechischen Religion* 1 (Munich, 1955).
"Pandemos"	E. Simon, "Aphrodite Pandemos auf attischen Münzen," *Schweizerische Numismatische Rundschau* 49 (1970) 5–19.
Parke	H. W. Parke, *Festivals of the Athenians* (London, 1977).
Pausanias	*Pausanias' Description of Greece* 1, trans. J. G. Frazer (London, 1898).
Pickard-Cambridge, *DFA*	A. Pickard-Cambridge, *The Dramatic Festivals of Athens*, rev. J. Gould and D. M. Lewis (2nd edition, Oxford, 1968).
Princeton Symposium	*Athens Comes of Age: From Solon to Salamis.* Papers of the Symposium Sponsored by the Archaeological Institute of America, The Princeton Society, and the Department of Art and Archaeology, Princeton University (Princeton, 1978).
Richardson, *Hymn*	*The Homeric Hymn to Demeter*, ed. N. J. Richardson (Oxford, 1974).

Schelp, *Kanoun*   J. Schelp, *Das Kanoun, der griechische Op-
                        ferkorb* (Würzburg, 1975).

Simon, *Götter*   E. Simon, *Die Götter der Griechen* (Munich,
                        1969).

Simon/Hirmer   E. Simon, M. Hirmer, and A. Hirmer, *Die
                        griechischen Vasen* (Munich, 1976).

Sokolowski, *LS*   F. Sokolowski, *Lois sacrées des cités grecques*
                        (Paris, 1969).

Thompson/Wycher-   H. A. Thompson and R. E. Wycherley, *The
ley   Athenian Agora* 14 (Princeton, 1972).

Toepffer, *AG*   I. Toepffer, *Attische Genealogie* (Berlin, 1889).

Wycherley   R. E. Wycherley, *The Stones of Athens*
                        (Princeton, 1978).

Ziehen   L. Ziehen, s.v. "Panathenaia," *RE* 18.3 (1949)
                        457–489.

Festivals of Attica

Introduction

The festivals of Athens are better known to us than the festivals of the other Greek states. The literary tradition is rich and so is that of the monuments, which range from modest Athenian vases to the Parthenon frieze. A treatment of Athenian festivals without the archaeological material would be incomplete, and so I shall refer frequently to the illustrations in the two main books on Attic festivals: Ludwig Deubner, *Attische Feste* (Berlin, 1932) and H. W. Parke, *Festivals of the Athenians* (London, 1977). These books were written by philologists, to whose field heortology (from Greek ἑορτή = festival) belongs. To understand the monuments, however, we need an archaeological approach of which Deubner makes greater use than Parke. The value of Parke's book, accordingly, is somewhat diminished, especially because the monuments date from the heyday of Attic festivals in the sixth, fifth, and fourth centuries B.C., whereas most of the literary evidence is considerably later.

In addition to ancient authors and Athenian works of art a third category of material is important for our purpose: the inscriptions. They tell us about the time and the form of festivals and (or) about the kind and the number of gifts for the gods. This epigraphical evidence is for the most part contemporary with the artistic monuments. It consists of public inscriptions on stone, which render an account of the cost of sacrifices, etc., because most of the Attic festivals were not private but public in character. We are here chiefly concerned with the state festivals and for this reason more private ceremonies are left out.[1]

The term "state festival" does not denote profane celebrations. All festivals of the polis were rooted in the cult of gods or heroes,[2] and were celebrated with religious rites. For that reason, Deubner's book is arranged by gods. We shall adopt a similar order here and shall not

---

1. Thus I do not speak here about the very Attic but more private veneration of herms; for it see Simon, *Götter* 307–9, pls. 294–97.

2. The state festivals for Attic heroes have been omitted; for them see Deubner 224–29; Kron passim; Parke 51–52, 81–82.

3

follow the order of Parke, who arranged the festivals according to the twelve months of the Athenian year. It is true that that arrangement is closer to Greek life. But the Athenian months seem extremely foreign to us. They correspond neither in chronology nor in name to our twelve months, which are based on the reform of the calendar by Julius Caesar and have the familiar Latin names. Later on the Roman months also came to Roman Greece, but until then each Greek polis had its own names of months—we know more than three hundred names.[3] The regions of Ionic, Aeolic, or Doric populations each have certain names of months in common, a fact that allows us to trace the migrations during the dark ages.[4]

The pre-Roman Greek months were lunar months lasting alternately twenty-nine and thirty days. In order to prevent these months from falling too far behind the solar year, leap years were necessary. The μέγας ἐνιαυτός consisted of a cycle of eight years of twelve months each, into which three additional months were fitted. Nilsson has shown that time-reckoning using the "great year" spread from Delphi all over Greece and that when nonlocal festivals such as the Olympic games or the Great Panathenaia occurred, the four-year cycle was based on the halved "great year."[5] In 776 B.C. therefore, the canonical date of the first Olympic festival and the starting point of dating by the Olympiads, the μέγας ἐνιαυτός was already established among the Greeks. The great authority of the Delphic oracle in the archaic period was based on Apollo's having measured out time for the Greek states. Among them Athens especially was linked to Delphi, and for this reason half of the Athenian months bear names referring to Apollo or his sister Artemis.[6] We shall deal with this again when we consider the festivals of these two gods.

The pre-Roman Attic year began in midsummer with Hekatombaion, the month of the greatest state festival, the Panathenaia. Other Greek communities also celebrated the festival of their main deity in

3. H. Bischoff, s.v. "Kalender," RE 10.2 (1919) 1575–1602; A. E. Samuel, Greek and Roman Chronology, Handbuch der Altertumswissenschaft I:7 (Munich, 1972) 57–138.

4. See infra pp. 75, 92.

5. Nilsson, GGR 644–47.

6. These months are Metageitnion, Boedromion, Pyanopsion, Elaphebolion, Mounychion, Thargelion: see Parke 51, 53, 73, 125, 137, 146; for Hekatombaion see infra n. 2 to chapter 4. For the Attic year see Samuel (supra n. 3) 57–63; for the problems involved: R. Meiggs and D. Lewis, A Selection of Greek Historical Inscriptions (Oxford, 1969) 171, 212–15, and passim.

the first month of their year.[7] Hekatombaion corresponds partly to July and partly to August and so on in the Attic calendar. These are the twelve Attic months:

Hekatombaion Metageitnion	summer
Boedromion Pyanopsion	fall
Maimakterion Poseideon Gamelion	winter
Anthesterion Elaphebolion Mounychion	spring
Thargelion Skiraphorion	summer

The Greeks liked personifications in cult, poetry, and the visual arts. For instance, they personified Demos ("the people") or Pompe ("the procession") or Olympias ("the Olympiad," pl. 5.1) or Kairos ("the opportune moment").[8] They also personified the months, whom they saw as young men. The heyday of personifications was the fourth century B.C. Towards the end of the first quarter of that century an Attic vase painter, named the Oinomaos Painter by Beazley, decorated a calyx-krater, fragments of which were found at Hermione in the Peloponnesos and are now in the National Museum in Athens (pl. 4). I have shown elsewhere that these fragments bear the first representations known to us of the Attic months.[9] They appear as young men clad in himatia and with the sickle of the moon above their heads. Some of them carry attributes of the festival which was celebrated in the course of the month they personify, and some are accompanied by girls who crown them. These may be named Pompai, personifications

7. So the first month in Delphi was Apellaios, with a festival of Apollo: Burkert, "Apellai" 10.

8. F. W. Hamdorf, *Griechische Kultpersonifikationen der vorhellenistischen Zeit* (Mainz, 1964) 30–32; Maass, *Prohedrie* 109 (Demos). Pompe is represented on a squat lekythos (Beazley, *ARV²* 1324.47) and on a chous (infra n. 10), both in the Metropolitan Museum, New York. The personification of the Olympiad occurs on the Panathenaic amphora Harvard 1925.30.124: Beazley, *Development* (2nd printing with corrections, 1964) 98–99, pl. 48.2 (here pl. 5.1). For Kairos see G. Schwarz, "Der Lysippische Kairos," *Grazer Beiträge* 4 (1975) 243–66.

9. "Monatsbilder" 105–23; other interpretations: S. Karouzou, *Deltion* 19 (1964) 1–16; Metzger 102–5, 120–21, pl. 46.

of the processions which, as we shall see, were a part of many festivals. The fragments of the Hermione krater are without inscriptions, but the famous Pompe on the Attic oinochoe in the Metropolitan Museum in New York of the same period is inscribed (pl. 5.2).[10]

Another representation of the Attic months is well known. They appear as youths or men in a frieze reused above the main entrance to the Little Metropolis, a Middle Byzantine church in Athens (pls. 1–3). Illustrated with a good commentary in Deubner,[11] it tells a lot about Athenian festivals. It needs a stylistic analysis because its date is not yet established, but there is no space to give to one here. I do not think that it was carved in the second or third century A.D. as Gerhard Rodenwaldt maintained.[12] With Hans Gundel and others I prefer a late Hellenistic date, perhaps in the middle of the first century B.C.[13] In its encyclopedic spirit this calendar-frieze seems related to the reliefs on the Tower of the Winds in Athens, which belong to that period. There is no trace of the cult of the Roman emperors, which would be inevitable if the frieze dated from the Empire. And last but not least, what are represented are the Athenian months and not the Roman ones.

The frieze consists of two blocks which were too long for the small Byzantine church. One was shortened on the left, and as a result the month Anthesterion was cut off. The other was shortened on the right, and part of the month Gamelion was cut off. It is a pity that each of them was not shortened on its other end, where there is an unfinished figureless zone. In the left half three Byzantine crosses were inserted; the central of these crosses obliterates the ship of the Panathenaic procession. How this frieze was originally used we do not know. But we can state that the representation did not begin with the first Attic month, Hekatombaion, which appears in the area of the aforesaid central cross. Hekatombaion is a young man clad in a himation and accompanied by Pompe, the personification of the procession at the Panathenaia.[14]

The sequence of the months in their new Byzantine context makes

10. No. 25.190. Metzger 66 No. 18, 60, with bibliography; Bömer, "Pompa" 1993–94; "Monatsbilder" 121, fig. 12; Schelp, *Kanoun* 27, 48. pl. 4.2; Simon/Hirmer pl. 235.

11. Deubner 248–54, pls. 34–40; "Monatsbilder" 112–15, figs. 6–10; Pickard-Cambridge *DFA* 51; H. Gundel, s.v. "Zodiakos," *RE* 10 A (1972) 623.

12. In Deubner 248.

13. F. Cumont in Deubner 248; Gundel (supra n. 11).

14. Deubner 250–51 following C. Robert called her Theoria, the personification of beholding. I have previously accepted this interpretation (see "Monatsbilder" 119–20), but Pompe now seems to me the better explanation; for Pompe see supra nn. 8, 10.

sense, because the year starts on the left with spring and ends on the right with winter. The Christian observers certainly did not understand the pagan festivals, but they understood the signs of the zodiac, which are likewise represented here.[15] They start with Aries on the left (pls. 1.1, 2.1). Taurus is destroyed by a cross. Gemini are two young men embracing. Above the sacrificial ox dedicated to Zeus Polieus—we shall soon return to it—appears Cancer (pls. 1.1, 2.2). To the right of the next cross Leo springs into the air. Virgo appears near Boedromion, and to the left of the third cross Libra is rendered in the shape of the claws of Scorpio (pls. 1.1, 2.3), which is shown in the right half of the frieze without them (pls. 1.2, 3.1). Sagittarius is the familiar centaur-archer and Capricorn is the forepart of a goat with a fishtail (pls. 1.2, 3.3). Aquarius and Pisces were cut off at either end when the frieze was reused. These signs surely helped to determine the proper sequence of the blocks and the order in which they have been preserved.

15. See Gundel (supra n. 11); as for Virgo and Libra, I do not follow Gundel, but prefer Deubner 253–54.

1

FESTIVALS OF ZEUS

Zeus with the epithet Herkeios was venerated together with Apollo Patroos by each Athenian citizen, as we know from Aristotle (*AP* 55). But this private cult does not concern us here; we can consider only the most important public cults of Zeus, and we begin with the oldest and strangest of all Athenian festivals, the Dipolieia.

DIPOLIEIA

The main sources for our knowledge about the Dipolieia are Pausanias (1.24.4) and the late antique author Porphyrios (*de abst*. 2.10 and 29–31), who uses Theophrastos. They are discussed by both Deubner and Parke,[1] but both disregard the archaeological material which has recently been discussed by Georgios Bakalakis.[2] Even more important for our understanding of the festival are a study by the Swiss ethnologist Karl Meuli[3] and Walter Burkert's *Homo Necans*.

The Dipolieia were celebrated in the last month of the Attic year, on 14 Skiraphorion, in honor of Zeus Polieus, the father and counterpart of the city-goddess Athena Polias. The festival was also called Bouphonia after the main rite, the slaying of an ox. It is represented in the calendar-frieze beneath the sign of Cancer (pl. 2.2). Beside Skiraphorion, who appears as a young athlete crowning himself, stands a bearded man with boots and a cloth around his waist. He holds a double ax above a tiny ox, the victim of the Bouphonia. The application of this name may seem surprising, because the slaying of animals

1. Deubner 158–74; A. B. Cook, *Zeus* 3 (Cambridge, 1940) 570–605; Nilsson, *GGR* 152–55; Parke 162–67; Burkert, *HN* 153–61; E. Simon, s.v. "Zeus," *RE* Suppl. 15 (1978) 1413–14; Melldahl/Flemberg 74–76.

2. "Das Zeusfest der Dipolieia auf einer Oinochoe in Saloniki," *AntK* 12 (1969) 56–60, following Cook (supra n. 1) 570–99, figs. 407–8.

3. "Griechische Opferbräuche" in *Phyllobolia für Peter Von der Mühll* (Basel, 1946) 185–88 = Meuli, *GesSch* 2:907–1018; the Dipolieia ibid., 1004–8 and passim.

was part of most Athenian state festivals. In spite of this, as we shall
see, the Bouphonia bear their name with good reason.

The priest of Zeus Polieus had a marble seat in the theater of Dionysos.[4] The temenos of Zeus Polieus was on the Acropolis northeast
of the Parthenon. Pausanias (1.24.4) mentions a statue of this god and
an altar. Excavation has revealed a small temple and an open-air precinct entered through a propylon, whose small central structure seems
to have been the place of the Dipolieia sacrifice.[5] Porphyrios speaks
not of an altar but of a bronze table. The altar of Zeus Polieus on the
Acropolis thus seems to have been a table-like structure and may have
been a relic of the Mycenaean age. A table is common place in representations of bull-offerings in Minoan and Mycenaean art, as Ioannis
Sakellarakis has shown in his study on the subject.[6] Not only are there
many gems and seal-impressions with a bull-victim on a table from
Crete and Mycenaean Greece (figs. 1a–d), there is also the Aghia Triada
sarcophagus with the bull on the offering table, bleeding to death.
Sakellarakis thinks this table was of wood, but it has the same yellow
color as the double axes on this sarcophagus, which were of metal.
Therefore the table may be metal, too, and would thus correspond to
Porphyrios' description of the altar of Zeus Polieus on the Acropolis.

At the festival, grain or cakes or both were placed on the table-altar
and oxen were driven around it. One of them would eat from the holy
things on the altar and therefore—so it was explained—would be killed
with a double ax (the πέλεκυς, a Bronze Age relic like the table), wielded
by a cult official called *bouphonos*.[7] Afterwards the bouphonos dropped
the ax and fled. The double ax was then brought to trial, cursed, and
thrown into the sea. The hide of the dead ox was stuffed to restore the
animal to the appearance of life. This in a few words recapitulates the
long account in Porphyrios, which in some details diverges from Pausanias. That Porphyrios preserves the better tradition is shown by several late black-figure Athenian vases studied by Bakalakis.[8] On these
vases a series of oxen—Pausanias speaks of only one ox—surround an

4. Maass, *Prohedrie* 104.

5. Judeich 257–58; G. P. Stevens, *The Setting of the Periclean Parthenon, Hesperia*
Suppl. 3 (Athens, 1940) 79–87; Travlos fig. 91, No. 118.

6. "Das Kuppelgrab A von Archanes und das kretisch-mykenische Tieropferritual,"
PZ 45 (1970) 166–98; the Aghia Triada sarcophagus ibid., 178–88; Sp. Marinatos and
M. Hirmer, *Kreta, Thera und das mykenische Hellas* (Munich, 1973) pl. XXXI; C. R.
Long, *The Ayia Triada Sarcophagus, SIMA* 41 (1974).

7. He was not identical with the priest mentioned supra n. 4, but was a cult official
from the clan of the Thaulonidai; see Toepffer, *AG* 149–60.

8. See supra n. 2; several vases with this decoration were collected in *ABL* 84–85,
and Bakalakis (supra n. 2) adds an oinochoe in Salonica, pl. 31.

Figures 1 a–d. Minoan-Mycenaean gems and seal-impressions with bull-offering, drawings; see p. 9. After *Prähist. Zeitschrift* 45 (1970) 169 figs. 5–8.

altar-like structure, and one of them stands on it, sometimes shown eating (pl. 6.1–3).[9] The white ox beneath may be a relief on the altar as Bakalakis thinks, perhaps may be the stuffed ox-hide of the previous Dipolieia,[10] or it may have been woven into a cloth covering the table-altar. In any case, the ox standing on the altar will be "punished" for eating the holy things, and afterwards the double ax will be punished for "murdering" the ox.

The slaying of the animal, then, was considered an injustice which needed expiation. Karl Meuli has shown that this conception goes back

9. Clearly visible on the oinochoe Munich J 1335 (here pl. 6); *ABL* No. 185; Beazley, *ABV* 473: Gela Painter. The structure is not a normal altar because the volutes are lacking.

10. The stuffed animal is perhaps represented on a hydria by the Nikoxenos Painter: Beazley, *ABV* 393.20; Parke fig. 63; Simon (supra n. 1) 1414; Melldahl/Flemberg 73–75, fig. 18, with a good critical commentary on this hydria which was on the Roman market in the last century and now seems to be lost.

to the customs of prehistoric hunting tribes. The rich ethnographic material collected by him indicates that the rites of the Attic Bouphonia reflect common customs of hunting people. Prehistoric man treated the game animal as his equal; he tried to ensure its goodwill by blaming other men or an object like the ax for killing it. He restored the form of the animal to secure its spirit and its return. He knew no gods, for they appeared at a relatively late stage of prehistoric cultural development, but he feared the spirits of the animals he had to kill for food.[11]

According to Parke, "Analogies have been sought with the practice of hunters placating the spirit of their dead prey. But this does not tally with a domestic animal as victim."[12] This is not convincing, however, because Parke's distinction between wild and domestic animals is an artificial one. Meuli showed that the agricultural tribes took over unchanged the rite of slaughtering animals from the hunting tribes and that this finally became the Olympian rite of immolation.[13] The thighbones, once preserved by the hunting people in order to restore the dead animal to life, were burned on the altar as an offering to the gods, and the meat was eaten by men.

The practice of ritual slaughter was thus continued from hunting tribes to agricultural communities and was one of the neolithic customs which still lingered in classical Athens; the festival was celebrated until late antiquity. In spite of all development in Greek thought and art, religious rites tended to be preserved pure and unchanged. Sometimes they were no longer understood; Aristophanes, for instance, makes jokes about the antiquated Dipolieia (*Clouds* 984). From the wording of Pausanias it follows that in his time the rite had taken on a mystic meaning. In mysteries, as we shall see in the festivals of Demeter, ancient traditions were safely preserved. Not the rite, but only the justification for it, was subject to evolution.

It is strange, therefore, that Deubner, followed by Parke, considers the Dipolieia a relatively young festival, instituted in the sixth century B.C.[14] Nobody in civilized archaic Athens could have invented that series of curious actions which correspond so closely to the ethnographic evidence collected by Meuli. Deubner's argument for a late date was based on the assumption that the cult of Athena on the Athe-

11. Meuli, *GesSch* 2: 948–80.

12. Parke 165.

13. Meuli, *GesSch* 2: 980–1012; Simon, *Götter* 149; W. Burkert, "Rešep-Figuren, Apollo von Amyklai und die 'Erfindung' des Opfers auf Cypern," *Grazer Beiträge* 4 (1975) 75–77.

14. Deubner 172–73; Parke 163–64.

nian Acropolis historically preceded the veneration of Zeus. This is by no means certain,[15] however, and therefore cannot contribute to a dating of the Dipolieia. As we have seen, the central act of ritual slaughter is considerably earlier than the worship not only of Zeus but also of Athena and all other Olympians. And it is probably not mere accident that the most ancient sacrifice of which we know is connected with the highest-ranking Greek god.

Apart from the official Bouphonia, Zeus Polieus received offerings from individual Attic demes. Thus the lengthy inscription of the deme Erchia speaks of a ram which was offered to this god in the month Skiraphorion (that is, at the Dipolieia), along with a ewe for Athena Polias.[16] But this was a deme-offering and not a polis-festival and therefore does not concern us here. We should like to know how Athena Polias took part in the Dipolieia, but there is no hint in the sources— though in the scholion to Aristophanes (*Clouds* 985) the Bouphonia are called Athena's festival.

DIASIA AND POMPAIA

In early spring, on 23 Anthesterion, the Diasia were celebrated, that is, the festival of Zeus.[17] It may have been represented in the calendar-frieze, but it is not preserved there because Anthesterion was cut off. Our main sources are Thucydides (1.126.6) and the inscription of Erchia already mentioned.[18] The latter is of the fourth century B.C., while Thucydides attests to the existence of the festival in the seventh century. But the Diasia must have been much older, considering the fact that a pre-Homeric Zeus was worshipped there. He had the epithet Meilichios, that is, "the friendly," a euphemistic name like Eumenides ("well-disposed ones") for the Erinyes or Asphalios ("the unshakeable one") for the earth-shaker Poseidon. Zeus Meilichios was not the Olympian king we know from Homer but an awe-

15. See infra Conclusions, pp. 106–7.

16. *SEG* 21, No. 541, cols. A and Γ, lines 61–64; Sokolowski, *LS* No. 18; Melldahl/Flemberg 75, n. 73, with bibliography; cf. also the offering for Zeus Polieus in Metageitnion, *SEG* 21, No. 541. col. Γ lines 15–18; Parke 179.

17. Deubner 155–57; M. Jameson, "Notes on the Sacred Calendar from Erchia," *BCH* 89 (1965) 159–72; Parke 120–22, 177–79; cf. also Jacoby's commentary on *FGrHist* 365 F 5.

18. Supra n. 16, col. A lines 38–43; for this calendar of deme offerings, the Greater Demarchia, see also G. Daux, "La Grande Démarchie: Un nouveau calendrier sacrificiel d'Attique (Erchia)," *BCH* 87 (1963) 603–34 and Jameson's article (supra n. 17).

some chthonic god who appeared as a big snake.[19] In votive reliefs
from the fourth century to Hellenistic times he may also be represented as a seated Zeus with a snake beside him or even without the
snake. Here Olympian traits are intruding, and the same can be observed in the later Diasia, as we shall see below.

In spite of his fearsome character, Zeus Meilichios was one of the
most popular gods of Attica and had many shrines in Athens and en-
virons.[20] According to Thucydides (1.126.6) his festival was called Διὸς
ἑορτὴ Μειλιχίου Μεγίστη, "the greatest festival of Zeus Meilichios,"
and this implies smaller celebrations for him apart from the Diasia.
Pausanias mentions an altar of Meilichios on the boundary between
Athenian and Eleusinian territory (1.37.4), but the main sanctuary for
the Diasia was on the banks of the river Ilissos. John Travlos in his
Topographical Dictionary of Ancient Athens did not indicate the sanctuary on the Ilissos, but it has been convincingly localized by Hans
Möbius and others near the so-called Ilissos Temple, where votives
for Zeus Meilichios have been found, and the Erchia inscription cor-
roborates this placement.[21]

The altar of Zeus Meilichios between Athens and Eleusis was located where Theseus was purified after his struggles against highway-
men and monsters on his way to Athens. For this reason some scholars
have seen in Zeus Meilichios a god who had to be appeased after
bloodshed. With such a restricted function, however, he would never
have gained the popularity he actually had in Athens. As a chthonic
deity he was angry by nature and had to be propitiated by everyone,
not just by murderers. So at the Diasia the whole populace brought
him bloodless offerings, θύματα ἐπιχώρια, as Thucydides (1.126.6)
says. The scholia explain these as cakes in the shape of animals, but
people may have also offered agricultural gifts such as grain and fruit,
because Meilichios, like many other chthonic gods, was connected

19. Nilsson, *GGR* 411–14. Votive reliefs for Zeus Meilichios: P. Foucart, "Bas-relief
du Pirée, le culte de Zeus Meilichios," *BCH* 7 (1883) 507–14, pl. 18 = Farnell 1:117,
pl. 2a = A. Rumpf, *Die Religion der Griechen. Bilderatlas zur Religionsgeschichte
XIII–XIV* (Leipzig, 1928) No. 25; U. Hausmann, *Griechische Weihreliefs* (Berlin, 1960)
80–83, 91, 97, pls. 47, 48, 57, 58; C. Blümel, *Die klassisch griechischen Skulpturen
der Staatlichen Museen zu Berlin* (Berlin, 1966) 75, No. 87, fig. 199 = Rumpf. ibid.,
No. 24.

20. Farnell 1:171–72; H. Schwabl, s.v. "Zeus" (Teil II), *RE* Suppl. 15 (1978) 1069–
71: eight different places of worship in Athens and Attica; Wycherley 189, 199, 265.

21. H. Möbius, "Das Metroon von Agrai und sein Fries," *AthMitt* 60/61 (1935/36)
256–57; Schwabl (supra n. 20) 1070; for the Ilissos temple see Judeich 420–21; Travlos
112–20; Wycherley 171. The identification is still open.

with the fertility of the soil. He sometimes carries a cornucopia[22], and he had a second festival in Athens, the Pompaia, the purpose of which was, as Deubner has proved, the magical protection of the newly sown grain.[23] The calendar-frieze does not show the procession of this festival, but it shows plowing and sowing, the main events of Maimakterion, in which the Pompaia took place (pl. 3.2). The skin of a ram which had been sacrificed to Meilichios and a caduceus, the staff with the twisted snakes, were carried in the procession, from which the festival took its name.

The Pompaia thus aid us in understanding the Diasia. Like many other Athenian festivals, both celebrations in honor of Zeus Meilichios were of rural origin, and I use the title "Festivals of Attica"—not of Athens—to emphasize this agricultural background. In fact the demes in which the Attic farmers lived took part in the Athenian Diasia, as we learn from the Erchia inscription.[24] They sent a ram to Athens, to the shrine of Meilichios on the banks of the river Ilissos. The sheepskin which was carried round at the Pompaia may have been taken from the ram offered the previous spring at the Diasia. Thus the two Athenian festivals of Meilichios, in the beginning of spring and in winter, would be closely connected. This is precisely the case with other agricultural festivals: we shall observe the same phenomenon in the cults of Demeter, Apollo, and Dionysos.

The ram of the deme Erchia was offered in an interesting mixture of chthonic and Olympian rites. The entrails were burned without using wine, a practice which corresponds to other chthonic cults; but the meat was eaten as in Olympian offerings. The tradition in Xenophon (*Anabasis* 7.8.4), where he speaks of whole burnt pigs for Meilichios, may or may not refer to the Diasia. We only know with certainty about the agricultural gifts mentioned by Thucydides and the mixed rite of the ram offering. Such a mixed rite is not unique in Greek religion[25] and can be explained by the nature of the god who was a chthonic being and, at the same time, Zeus.

As we know from Aristophanes' *Clouds* (408–9), the Diasia were famous for their meals; according to the same source there were also

22. Thus in the votive relief Parke fig. 48, showing a family offering a pig.

23. Deubner 157–58; Bömer, "Pompa" 1958, No. 220; Parke 95–96; Schwabl (supra n. 20) 1069.

24. Supra n. 18. For the fleece see Deubner 49; P. Stengel, s.v. "Διὸς κώδιον," *RE* 5:1 (1903) 1084; Richardson, *Hymn* 212–13.

25. See F. Pfister, "Studien zum homerischen Epos: Epos und Heroenkult," *WürzJbb* 3 (1948) 147–53 = K. v. See, "Europäische Heldendichtung," *WDF* 500 (1978) 105–14; U. Kron, "Zum Hypogäum von Paestum," *JdI* 86 (1971) 145–47.

Figure 2. Votive relief with man and child in front of a big snake, probably Zeus Meilichios. Berlin (east); see p. 15. After C. Blümel (see n. 27 to chapter 1) pl. 77.

gifts for children (864). This fits, as Deubner writes, into the cheerful side of the popular festival, but I think the significance was deeper. Chthonic deities like Demeter, the Nymphs, or Meilichios, who was also venerated in the newly discovered sanctuary of the Nymphs near the Acropolis,[26] had a special affection for children; they were tutelary gods for them. Votive-offering scenes that include children therefore often turn up where chthonic gods were worshipped. I shall mention only one example here: a votive relief of the early fourth century B.C. in Berlin, said to be from Boeotia (fig. 2).[27] It shows a big snake, rightly interpreted as Meilichios, to whom a man and a child are praying.

OLYMPIEIA

We learn from Lucian (*Icarom.* 24) that the Diasia were abandoned in the second century after Christ. This may have been caused by the completion of the nearby Olympieion under the emperor Hadrian. The god of this giant temple, Zeus Olympios, seems to have overlapped the chthonic cult of Zeus Meilichios in that region. Zeus Olympios was the Homeric king of gods and men, whose festival, the

26. Schwabl (supra n. 20) 1070; Wycherley 199–200. Chthonic gods protecting children: Hadzisteliou Price 128 and passim.

27. C. Blümel, *Katalog der griechischen Skulpturen des 5. und 4. Jhs. v. Chr.* (Berlin, 1928) 65–66, K 92, pl. 77 = Blümel (supra n. 19) 65, No. 74, fig. 111.

Olympieia, the sons of Peisistratos had probably founded.[28] In any case the Peisistratids had laid the foundations of the temple. The Olympieia were celebrated towards the end of spring, on 19 Mouny-chion, and were dedicated more to sports than to religious rites. The main attractions seem to have been horse races in the Hippodrome and other performances involving horses. Hadrian endowed the festival with agonistic games, in addition to completing the temple after seven centuries. So the interest in the cult of Zeus Meilichios may have faded, as chthonic cults in general faded in imperial times, the heyday of astral religion.

THEOGAMIA

The last festival of Zeus to be considered here was a festival of Hera as well, because it was their ἱερὸς γάμος, the sacred wedding.[29] The cult of Hera was not strongly rooted in Attica. As in Homeric poetry, in cult the goddess was also the great mistress of Argos. The wedding of Zeus and Hera was celebrated towards the end of the month Gamelion, which was named after this festival. The literary sources discussed by Deubner are sparse and half of the wedding scene was cut off in the calendar frieze (pl. 3.3). We see only the bride; the bridegroom is not preserved. Deubner thinks this veiled figure represents a mortal bride. It seems possible, however, that she is Hera herself, because there are, as we shall see, other deities in the frieze, for instance Artemis (pl. 2.1). If the bride is Hera, the bridegroom must have been Zeus. The most beautiful reflection of this festival is to be found in another context, in the group of Zeus and Hera in the east frieze of the Parthenon.

28. Deubner 177; Parke 144. For the Olympieion see Judeich 382–84; Travlos 402–11; Wycherley 155–66; T. Leslie Shear, Jr., "Tyrants and Buildings in Archaic Athens," Princeton Symposium 10.
29. Deubner 177–78; Parke 104. Zeus and Hera in the Parthenon frieze: Brommer, *PF* pl. 174.

2

FESTIVALS OF DEMETER

Cults of Demeter were widespread in Greece, and many of them were mystery cults. The oldest of them were the Thesmophoria, the most celebrated of Greek festivals, found all over Greece.[1] The most important sanctuary of Demeter was at Eleusis, where the Great Mysteries took place; these were of Mycenaean origin and became an Athenian state festival in the sixth century B.C. The Mysteries were celebrated by both men and women, but most of the other festivals of Demeter were exclusively for women; thus, before discussing the festivals of Demeter in detail, we first must ask why this is so.

The female worshippers of Demeter correspond with the Roman matrons who celebrated—also with secret rites—the festival of Bona Dea.[2] Common features in cults of ancient Greece and Rome can often be explained by their great antiquity, and this applies here. A long time ago Jane Harrison convincingly showed that the Thesmophoria and other women's festivals could be explained by the customs of a neolithic society in which women cared for the crops.[3] Her method of interpreting certain rites in social terms is followed in our time by many scholars, for instance by Burkert. In criticizing Harrison, Farnell and Nilsson have argued that in Minoan Crete and in Mycenaean Greece plowing and sowing had already become male occupations. This is true, but the rites of the festivals in question here had their origin not in the Bronze Age but in much earlier prehistoric times. They were rooted in the Neolithic, when grain-growing and hog-raising, new inventions then, were done by women. Therefore women, crops, and piglets remained connected in the Thesmophoric rite. As we have seen in the Dipolieia, the neolithic practice of killing animals

1. Nilsson, *GF* 313–25; Nilsson, *GGR* 461–66.
2. K. Latte, *Römische Religionsgeschichte*, Handbuch der Altertumswissenschaft 5.4: (Munich, 1960) 230–31.
3. J. E. Harrison, *Prolegomena to the Study of Greek Religion*[3] (Cambridge and New York, 1922) 272; cf. Nilsson, *GF* 323; Farnell 4:106; Nilsson, *GGR* 465. For Harrison's sociological method see Burkert, "Apellai" 12.

17

sacrally lingered in classical Athens. The same happened to imme-
morial practices in Demeter's cult.

THESMOPHORIA AND STENIA

These festivals took place in the fall, in the second week of Pyanopsion,[4] a month which in Boeotia and elsewhere was called Deme-
trios. Both were closely connected and were celebrated exclusively by
women. The importance of the Thesmophoria emerges from the fact
that they lasted three days. The first day was called *Anodos* ("ascent")
because the sanctuary of Demeter was situated on a hill. This was the
case not only in Athens but everywhere in Greece and among the
Western Greeks in Italy and Sicily. During the three days of the festival the participants lived in the sanctuary; they built huts there in
which they sat and where they slept on the ground. The second day
was called *Nesteia* ("fast"), because the celebrants abstained from food,
a practice known from many cults as a preparation for the main rite.
The third day was called *Kalligeneia*, which means "beautiful offspring," and which was also the name of a goddess invoked at the
Thesmophoria.

We do not know much more about this festival because its rites were
strictly secret. Aristophanes in his comedy *The Women at the Thesmophoria* does not reveal cult practices. He takes the second day of
the festival, however, as an ideal occasion to show women by themselves and to make fun of this. As we learn from the *Thesmophoriazousai* (658 and scholia to 624) the Thesmophorion of Athens was on
the hillside of the Pnyx, where it has been tentatively identified by
Homer Thompson.[5] In the calendar-frieze a woman with a large round
basket (*kiste*) on her head stands in the month Pyanopsion and therefore must represent the Thesmophoria (pl. 3.1). Similar *kistaphoroi*
are known from the Eleusinian propylon of the first century B.C.[6] The
triglyphs of the same building are ornamented with ears of grain and
kistai. These were the containers of the secret objects used in mystery
cults. The woman in the calendar-frieze carries in the kiste the mys-

4. Deubner 50–60; Parke 82–88.
5. H. A. Thompson, "Pnyx and Thesmophorion," *Hesperia* 5 (1936) 151–200; see
Judeich 398–99. Travlos 198, following Broneer, calls a structure near the Eleusinion
the Thesmophorion; see Thompson/Wycherley 152, n. 178. But Aristophanes' women
are certainly on the Pnyx. There may have been several Thesmophoria in a large city
like Athens; for the Piraeus see Sokolowski, *LS* No. 36.
6. Mylonas 159, pl. 56; the triglyphs ibid., pl. 57.

terious things of the Thesmophoria. As Nilsson, Deubner, and others have shown, they were called ϑεσμοί ("things laid down") and they gave the name to the festival. From Homer onwards this word in Greek literature is used to mean "laws" and therefore scholars have frequently explained Demeter Thesmophoros as a law-giving goddess.[7] Because the Thesmophoria are older than Homer, however, we must see that she was evidently not named after the idea of law but after the festival; therefore the epithet is to be explained by the rites of the Thesmophoria.

The main source for the action shown in the calendar-frieze is a scholion to Lucian (*dial. mer.* 2.1), which, however, is confused, and Deubner's interpretation, followed by Nilsson and Parke but not by Homer Thompson, remains hypothetical.[8] The text speaks of piglets and cakes which were thrown into caves; as excavations have revealed, such caves are found in most sanctuaries of Demeter. Later on women called *Antletriai* ("bailers") went down to the caves to retrieve the putrefied remains and put them on the two altars—for Demeter and Persephone—in the Thesmophorion. Deubner is surely right in calling the remains of piglets and cakes *thesmoi*, because they had been "laid down" previously, in the caves. The scholion does not say on which day of the Thesmophoria the thesmoi were retrieved by the women. Deubner and Parke think it was the second day, but this was a day of abstinence and preparation for the main rite, the carrying of the thesmoi from the caves to the altars. It seems more likely that they were brought up from the caves immediately before they were needed, that is, in the night between the second day and the last, a night that, according to ancient time-reckoning, would have belonged to the third day of the festival, the Kalligeneia.[9]

The scholion to Lucian similarly does not specify the time when the piglets and cakes were thrown into the caves. For this rite Deubner suggested the festival Skira in the month Skiraphorion. As we shall see, the Skira was definitely a festival of Demeter; but it is questionable whether any piglets and cakes would have remained after four months, for in the Greek summer they would have decayed very quickly or have been eaten by scavengers. Therefore, I give here a new hypothesis. Two days before the Thesmophoria were celebrated, on 9

7. See, e.g., U. v. Wilamowitz-Moellendorff, *Der Glaube der Hellenen* 1 (1931) 204; *LSJ* 795.

8. Deubner 40–44, 50–51; Nilsson, *GGR* 463; Parke 83; earlier I followed Deubner (Simon, *Götter* 92), whereas Thompson (supra n. 5, 188 n. 1) rightly doubts Deubner's reconstruction.

9. For this time-reckoning see Deubner 93 with n. 3.

Pyanopsion, Athenian women assembled for the Stenia, another strictly
female festival of Demeter.[10] It is mentioned in the *Thesmophoriazousai* (834 with scholia). We know only that it was a nocturnal festival in
which the women mutually insulted each other. Grumbling and scoff-
ing occur frequently in cults of Demeter, to divert the goddess from
her grief for her daughter (the episode with Iambe in the Homeric
hymn to Demeter had the same purpose),[11] but this was never the
main rite of a festival. Therefore I think that the piglets and other
things were thrown down during the night of the Stenia to be retrieved a few days later during the night of the Kalligeneia and taken
to the altars.

Deubner thinks this rite, which he connects with the Skira, is represented on a red-figure lekythos.[12] A young woman bends forward
holding a basket for offerings (*kanoun*) in her left hand and in her right
an animal. Before her three torches stand in the soil. The attitude of
the woman certainly indicates that she is about to throw the animal
into the depths. This, however, is not a piglet but a dog, as we see by
the head, the legs, and the tail. Dogs were offered to Hekate, a goddess connected with the Underworld. The three torches also evoke
this goddess, who was represented in threefold shape. An offering to
Hekate makes sense on a lekythos, because these vases were used in
the cult of the dead.

Bernard Ashmole has tentatively identified a scene on an Attic cup
of the Siana type in London as a festival for Demeter, perhaps, he
thinks, the third day of the Thesmophoria.[13] Five women and a boy
are dancing around an altar, where a priestess with a *liknon* stands.
On the left Demeter sits mourning on a chair. This picture, of the
second quarter of the sixth century B.C., definitely shows a dance in
honor of the goddess to cheer her up in her grief, but I think it is not
a secret rite. Demeter also had a series of smaller festivals in Attica,[14]
for instance the Chloia or the Haloa; the latter we shall consider at the
end of this chapter. One of these is probably represented in the scene

10. Deubner 52–53; Parke 88, 188.

11. For this episode and generally for αἰσχρολογία in Demeter's cult see Richardson, *Hymn* 213–17.

12. Athens, Nat. Mus. 1695 (C.C.1428). Deubner 44, pl. 2; Beazley *ARV²* 1204.2:
connected with the Group of Palermo 16. Deubner's interpretation was refuted by A.
Rumpf, "Attische Feste-Attische Vasen," *BonnJbb* 161 (1961) 208–9, who showed that
this is an offering to Genetyllis or Hekate.

13. London 1906.12–15.1. B. Ashmole, "Kalligeneia and Hieros Arotos," *JHS* 66
(1946) 8–10, pls. 2–3; Beazley, *ABV* 90.7: Burgon Group; C. Bérard, "Le Liknon
d'Athéna," *AntK* 19 (1976) 102, pl. 27.1.

14. See Deubner 67–69; Parke 149.

on this cup. The frieze on the other side of the cup shows a stout man plowing and a young man sowing (pl. 7.1). They do Δήμητρος ἔργα, the works of Demeter, as farmers' work was called.[15] The goddess had taught agriculture to mankind—and first of all (so the Athenians believed) to the people of Attica. Bouzyges, the ancestor of the Bouzygai, an Athenian clan, was the first to plow. Therefore members of this clan performed the ἱερὸς ἄροτος, the sacred plowing, each year at the foot of the Acropolis.

According to Ashmole, the sacred plowing is represented on the London cup; and according to Deubner it is also represented in the calendar-frieze in the month Maimakterion (pl. 3.2). The most beautiful representation is on a classical bell-krater in the Fogg Art Museum (pl. 7.2).[16] Here Kekrops and Demeter herself with scepter and ears of grain look on, while the ancestor of the Bouzygai plows with two oxen. On this krater and on the London cup the naked hero Bouzyges is shown,[17] whereas the plowman in the calendar-frieze in his priestly garment is a member of the Bouzygai. There are many other representations of Demeter and Kore, especially in the farewell scene with Triptolemos,[18] but there exists no visual document showing the rites of the Thesmophoria. This is not surprising: no artist could have watched the women or dared to represent their secret rites.

The sense of the Thesmophoria becomes apparent from the name of the last day, Kalligeneia. It was celebrated to convey fertility to the soil and to married women. The thesmoi were taken from the altars in the Thesmophorion and mixed with the grain to be sown towards the end of Pyanopsion and—as the calendar-frieze shows (pl. 3.2)—in the following month, Maimakterion. The piglets and cakes no doubt served as a fertility charm, but I think we must ask why this charm had to be

15. Hesiod, *Erga* 393; see the commentary by M. L. West, *Hesiod. Works and Days* (Oxford, 1978) 258; for ancient representations see A. S. F. Gow, "The Ancient Plough," *JHS* 34 (1914) 249–75.

16. Inv. 60.345, from Vari. *CVA* USA 6 Robinson Coll. 2 (1937) pl. 48.2; Beazley, *ARV²* 1115.30: Hephaistos Painter; Kron 95–96, pl. 12.1. Kron interprets the goddess with the ears of grain as Athena; I follow Beazley, who saw in her "perhaps Demeter," because the tree is not certainly an olive and the "lance" of the goddess looks more like a scepter.

17. It is true that nakedness was typical for the "works of Demeter" (see Hesiod, *Erga* 391–92): but the size of the plowman on the London cup (supra n. 13) and his onlookers on the bell-krater show that he is a hero. For Bouzyges and the Bouzygai see Toepffer, *AG* 136–49; for Perikles (ibid. 147–48) cf. however Davies, *APF* 459.

18. See "La mission de Triptolème d'après l'imagerie athénienne," *Recueil Ch. Dugas* (Paris, 1960) 123–39, pls. XXVII–XXXIV; additions: A. Peschlow-Bindokat, "Demeter und Persephone in der attischen Kunst des 6. bis der 4. Jahrhunderts," *JdI* 87 (1972) 146–47; cf. Graf, *Eleusis* 176.

putrefied. Would not a pomegranate, which modern Greek farmers throw with the first-sown grain,[19] have fulfilled the same purpose? It seems probable to me that the thesmoi reflect a great invention of prehistoric grain-growing settled people: fertilizing by means of compost. As we know from Homer (*Od.* 17.297ff.), composting was practiced on the farm of Odysseus.[20] On his return the hero finds his famous poor dog sitting before the doors of the palace on dung of mules and cows "with which," Homer says, "the farmworkers fertilize the property of Odysseus." As Demeter was the goddess of agriculture, the belief that she was also connected with fertilizing the soil is not absurd. In any case, the concrete meaning of thesmoi, which antedates the abstract meaning "laws," may well have been "compost heaps," because the fertilizing material had to be "laid down" for a while before it was used on the fields.

SKIRA

The third festival of Demeter celebrated exclusively by women, the Skira, took place two days before the Dipolieia.[21] In Greece this is the time when grain is cut and threshed and therefore Demeter, the giver of crops, had to be venerated. Like the Thesmophoria the Skira was a festival of women, and was celebrated with secret rites, about which we know nothing. Piglets may have been thrown into Demeter's sacred caves, because they were favorite offerings in her cult. But as I have shown above, these were not the piglets whose remains were retrieved at the Thesmophoria.

The etymology of Skira was already a matter of dispute in antiquity. Because Athena in Salamis (Herodotus 8.94) and Phaleron (Pausanias 1.1.4) bore the epithet Skiras, the festival was also thought—by both ancient and modern scholars—to be essentially hers.[22] In fact Athena took part in it, but as Athena Polias and in honor of Demeter, as we shall see.

Parke maintains that, because of the polytheistic structure of Greek religion, several deities would sometimes be involved in the same fes-

---

19. Deubner 51–52.

20. See W. Richter, "Die Landwirtschaft im homerischen Zeitalter," *ArchHom* II:H (1968) 104–5.

21. F. Pfister, s.v. "Skira," *RE* 3 A 1 (1927) 530–33; Deubner 40–50; Burkert, *HN* 161–68; Parke 156–58.

22. Deubner 45 n. 6; for Athena *Skiras*, the goddess of the Salaminioi, see Ferguson 18–20, 28; Kron 172.

tival. This is generally true, though there usually is a special reason. I will try to show this for the Skira. It is unfortunate that the work of Lysimachides, an author probably of the Augustan period, who wrote about the months and festivals of Athens, is almost completely lost. Only a few passages of his heortology are given by later authors (*FGrHist* 366 F1 0). Among them is an interesting detail about the Skira (F3). On that day, we learn from Lysimachides, the priestess of Athena, the priest of Poseidon, and the priest of Helios walked beneath a big sunshade, because it was a hot summer day, to a place called Skiron, and this procession was ushered by the Eteoboutadai. This was an ancient clan, believed to be descended from the Athenian kings.[23] Even in democratic Athens the priestess of Athena *Polias* and the priest of Poseidon always came from this distinguished clan. As Lysimachides attests, there was also a priest of the sun god among the Eteoboutadai. Because there is no other testimony for a priest of Helios in archaic and classical Athens, the passage was considered by Deubner to be apocryphal and regarded by Parke as a riddle. But because our knowledge of Athenian cults is far from complete, we should take Lysimachides seriously. The clan of the Eteoboutadai, who before Kleisthenes' reform were simply called Boutadai, dated back to the time of the Athenian kings in the Bronze Age. As we know from representations in art and from several myths, the sun was held in high esteem in Bronze Age religion. Think of the big gold ring from Tiryns with the cult scene and the celestial bodies above,[24] or think of the story about Helios and his flocks in the *Odyssey*. The veneration of Helios seems to have lingered in that aristocratic clan from Mycenaean to classical times and may even have been the reason why Helios so often appears in works of art of the Periclean age. The Eteoboutadai, who held the priesthood of Athena Polias, certainly had an influence on the sculptural program of the Parthenon and on the statue of Athena Parthenos.

But to return to the Σκίρα: Why did the Eteoboutadai go on that day to Σκῖρον, a place with rocks of white limestone?[25] By analogy to other Greek festivals, an important rite must have been performed there. Skiron was near the Kephissos, the boundary between Athenian and Eleusinian territory (Pausanias 1.36.4). I have already men-

23. Toepffer, *AG* 113–33; Davies, *APF* 348–53.

24. Marinatos and Hirmer (supra n. 6 to chapter 1) pl. 229.1; cf. ibid. the gold ring from Mycenae: pl. 229.2 (here pl. 14.1).

25. The iota is long in the place name, whereas in the name of the festival it is short (see Deubner 46, n. 11). Therefore the etymology of Skira and of the month-name Skiraphorion remains dark.

tioned the altar of Zeus Meilichios there (supra, p. 13). Pausanias
mentions a sanctuary of Demeter, Kore, Athena, and Poseidon in the
same region (1.37.2). This sounds like a compromise arranged between Athenian and Eleusinian cults. According to Deubner the
Eteoboutadai went to this sanctuary of Demeter at Skiron, and I think
there is no better hypothesis. By the procession of the noblest of all
Athenian clans to the boundaries of Eleusis, Demeter was especially
honored. The compromise between the cults of the two poleis certainly was due to a religious contract between Athens and Eleusis,
which was renewed every year at Demeter's festival. Contracts used
to be accompanied by an oath, and for this reason, I think, the priest
of Helios was present. Helios was one of the most important Greek
oath-gods, as we know, for example, from his role in the oath between
Achaeans and Trojans in the third book of the *Iliad* (277).

Finally, the priest of Poseidon accompanied the priestess of Athena
Polias not only because they belonged to the same clan, but also because Poseidon, who was worshipped along with Demeter, Kore, and
Athena in the same border sanctuary, had close relations with Eleusis.
He had a temple there as Poseidon Pater (Pausanias 1.38.6) and he
was the ancestor of the most distinguished Eleusinian clan, the Eumolpidai.[26] Perhaps the highest priest of Eleusis, the hierophant, who
was a Eumolpid, met the noble Athenian priests in the sanctuary to
renew the contract. But there are no literary sources for this sugges-
tion.

THE GREAT MYSTERIES

This festival lasted the whole third week of Boedromion and into
the fourth week.[27] Together with the Panathenaia and the City Dionysia it made up the triad of the greatest Athenian festivals. In later
times, especially after the second half of the fourth century B.C., it
attracted people from far abroad and remained, after the Olympic
games, the most famous Greek festival until late antiquity. At that
time it was a serious rival of Christianity, and Christians were the first
to betray the sacral secrets of the Mysteries. But their accounts are so
mixed with polemics that little can be gathered from them for our
purpose.

26. Toepffer, *AG* 24–80; Maass, *Prohedrie* 124; Richardson, *Hymn* 197–98.
27. Deubner, 69–91; Nilsson, *GGR* 653–67; Simon, *Götter* 97–117; Bömer, "Pompa"
1931–32; Richardson, *Hymn* 12–30 and passim; Parke 55–72.

Excavations of the Greek Archaeological Society in the Eleusinian sanctuary have shown that a shrine already existed there in the Mycenaean period, and the importance of the site at that time is attested by the big Bronze Age necropolis nearby.[28] In the Homeric hymn to Demeter, one of our main sources for the Eleusinian cult, the Mycenaean background is apparent. This fine piece of poetry gives an account of the events which led to the origin of the Mysteries. Its central theme is the rape of Kore-Persephone by Hades. Of course neither the hymn nor any other source before the Christian authors touches themes which were forbidden; silence regarding all secret religious rites, not only those of Eleusis, was maintained throughout antiquity. Pausanias does not even describe the architecture of the Eleusinian sanctuary (cf. 1.38.7). But this degree of reticence approaches superstition, because not everything connected with the cult was subject to concealment. The procession of the *mystai* to Eleusis, their songs, the attributes and offerings they carried, could be seen or heard by everyone.[29] Only the contents of the sacred kistai and the experiences of the mystai in the sanctuary during the initiation were secret. If more had been forbidden, Demeter and the figures of her circle could not have been, as they were, one of the favorite themes of Attic art.[30]

It seems to me that in the calendar-frieze the Eleusinian Mysteries are indicated (pl. 2.3). The month Boedromion, a young man clad in a himation, is accompanied by a young rider. Deubner thought that he was a cavalryman exercising.[31] But because there are no other profane representations in the frieze, it makes better sense to see him in a ritual context. We know that on 13 and 14 Boedromion, the days before the Mysteries began, Athenian ephebes, that is, young men in military training, escorted τὰ ἱερά ("The Holy Things") from Eleusis to Athens. They were brought to the Eleusinion at the foot of the Acropolis, which has been excavated by American scholars.[32] The galloping rider in the frieze seems to me to be one of the ephebes in charge of escorting the Holy Things which were certainly hidden in kistai.[33]

After τὰ ἱερά were received in the Eleusinion, one of the cult per-

---

28. G. E. Mylonas, *Τὸ δυτικὸν νεκροταφεῖον τῆς Ἐλευσῖνος* (Athens, 1975).

29. See Graf, *Eleusis* 50 with n. 47.

30. Peschlow-Bindokat (supra n. 18) 60–157.

31. Deubner 254; perhaps in the large unfinished zone which begins beside the rider, the procession of the *mystai* was planned.

32. Travlos 198–203; Thompson/Wycherley 150–55.

33. For these round baskets, used also at the Thesmophoria, see supra n. 6. They were carried by priestesses (ἱερεῖαι); see sources in Bömer, "Pompa" 1931.

sonnel went up to the Acropolis and reported their arrival to the
priestess of Athena Polias. Parke writes: "By this charming piece of
etiquette the senior importance of the city's goddess over all other
divinities was maintained in dignity."[34] As we have seen, at the Skira
festival Athena's priestess went to Demeter; now, at the beginning of
the Mysteries, Demeter comes to Athena. These respectful relations
between the two goddesses go back in part to the sixth century B.C.,
when the Eleusinian Mysteries became an Athenian state festival, but
they may partly antedate the annexation of Eleusis by Athens, for the
following reasons: Athena was the palace goddess of the Mycenaean
kings of Athens, and those kings were responsible for the well–being
of their populace, who would blame them for a bad harvest. At the
beginning of Sophokles' *Oidipus Tyrannos* this concept is clearly artic-
ulated. The palace goddess needed Demeter's help to prevent hungry
years for her kings and the whole population.

The Great Mysteries properly began with the full moon on 15 Boedromion, a day which was called *Agyrmos* ("gathering") because the
mystai-to-be assembled in the Stoa Poikile in the Athenian Agora.
They were permitted to attend the Great Mysteries only if they had
previously been initiated into the Lesser Mysteries of Agrai (then a
village southeast of Athens). Therefore we must consider briefly that
earlier celebration.[35]

For some time scholars believed that the so-called Ilissos Temple
was the "Metroon in Agrai" where the Lesser Mysteries took place.
Recently Travlos, Wycherley, and others have preferred to call it the
temple of Artemis Agrotera, because they believe that the foundations
of the Metroon are found nearby on the Ilissos.[36] The problem cannot
be solved here, but another point regarding the Metroon is important
for the festival. This was not, as Nilsson, Parke, and many others write,[37]
a temple of Demeter but of Rhea, Mother of the Gods, who in Athens
was simply called Mother. Her cult was long established there and
she had several sanctuaries, one of them in the Agora. Countless reliefs with Rhea on a throne with *tympanon* and lion have turned up in
Athens, many of them of poor quality, but testifying to the popularity

34. Parke 60.
35. Deubner 70; Nilsson, *GGR* 667–69; Jameson (supra n. 17 to chapter 1) 159–62;
"EleusD" 83–85; Graf, *Eleusis* 66–78; Parke 58, 122–24.
36. See n. 21 to chapter 1.
37. Nilsson, *GGR* 668; Parke 58; Wycherley (171) writes: "here the Mother and
Demeter were apparently identified." As far as I know, the two goddesses were sometimes identified in poetry but not in Athenian cult; for the problem see R. Kannicht,
Euripides' Helena 2 (Heidelberg, 1969) 329–30; Richardson, *Hymn* 295–96.

of that goddess, who for the Athenians was not Demeter but her mother, as she was the mother of Zeus and other Olympians. Her role in the Eleusinian Mysteries is well defined in the Homeric hymn to Demeter (441–69): After the abduction of Kore, the Mother of the Gods alone succeeds in reconciling Demeter with gods and men. The reconciliation is represented, as I have shown elsewhere, on the so called Eleusinian pelike in Leningrad (pl. 8.2),[38] and a similar representation of the triad Demeter-Kore-Rhea with Ploutos and Triptolemos occurs on a hydria of the Kerch style in the Abegg-Stiftung Bern, which is shown here for the first time (pl. 9)[39]. Without Rhea's intervention Demeter would not be appeased and the Mysteries, the consequence of the pacification, would not exist. From this point of view it is quite natural that the Metroon was the first step on the road to initiation. The rites of Agrai were, like the rites of Eleusis, secret and are therefore unknown to us. In any case, they were clearly prerequisites for the Eleusinian Mysteries.

The first four days of the Great Mysteries were celebrated in Athens, while the Holy Things were housed in the Eleusinion at the foot of the Acropolis. We know from Aristotle that the *archon basileus* (the king archon), one of the three highest Athenian officials, superintended the festival, and that he had four helpers, "two from the citizen body as a whole, one from the clan of the Eumolpidai, and one from the clan of the Kerykes" (*AP* 57). These were the two ancient clans of Eleusis, which until late antiquity supplied the two main priesthoods of the Mysteries: the hierophant and the *dadouchos*.[40] We know their appearance mainly from a series of vase-paintings.

On vases of the rich and Kerch styles they usually wear an *ependytes* (an ornamented tunic for cult purposes) and high Thracian boots, and carry one or two torches. Generally, the ancestors of the two Athenian clans, Eumolpos and (or) Keryx, are shown rather than the Athenian officials because the scenes take place in mythical times. Thus Eumolpos appears with ependytes, torches, and Thracian boots on the Eleusinian pelike which belongs to the ripe Kerch style (pl.

38. St. 1792, from Kerch. FR pl. 70; Beazley, *ARV*[2] 1476.1: Eleusinian Painter; Metzger 40, No. 35, pl. 24; "EleusD" 72–78, pls. 17, 19.1; Graf, *Eleusis* 64; Bianchi 16–17, Nos. 1, 2.

39. Rhea, here also seated on an *omphalos*, is speaking, whereas on the pelike (pl. 8.2) she is listening to Demeter. The Abegg hydria (height 46.5 cm.) is shown here with the kind permission of Mr. Abegg and Mr. Stettler.

40. For the Eumolpidai see supra n. 26; for the Kerykes: Toepffer, *AG* 80–92; Ferguson 23–24; Davies, *APF* 254–71. Generally: K. Clinton, "The Sacred Officials of the Eleusinian Mysteries," *TAPS* 64.3 (1974).

8.2; Fig. 3b). Eumolpos is similarly dressed on the "Regina Vasorum,"
an Attic relief-hydria from Cumae in Leningrad (pl. 10.1),[41] and on a
squat lekythos of the late rich style which shows the reunion of Demeter and Kore.[42] A similar figure on the fragment from the circle of
Meidias in the Museum of Fine Arts in Boston bears the inscription
"Eumolpos."[43] On vases of the first half of the fifth century he is not a
youth but is bearded, for instance on the skyphos by Hieron and Makron in London, where he sits beneath one handle and is identified
by an inscription (fig. 3a).[44] His attribute here is Apollo's swan, a musical animal, because the name of Eumolpos comes from εὖ μέλπεσθαι
("to sing beautifully"). On a skyphos in Brussels of the second quarter
of the fifth century Eumolpos still wears normal dress, chiton and
himation.[45] He stands with two torches between Herakles and Iolaos,
who carry the attribute of Eleusinian mystai, the *bakchos*.

The initiation of Herakles was a favorite theme of Athenian art, not
only for religious but also for political reasons. The same may be said
about the Dioskouroi who sometimes join Herakles as mystai (pl. 8.1).[46]
Thus the main heroes of the Peloponnesos are shown closely connected with Athens. They had even become Athenian citizens, because otherwise they could not have been initiated.[47] This requirement

41. Eleusinian Pelike: supra n. 38. "Regina Vasorum": Leningrad 51659, from Cumae. Metzger 40–41, No. 36, pls. 20–22, with bibliography; "EleusD" 84–85, 89–90;
Graf, *Eleusis* 62–64; Bianchi 17–18, No. 5. According to M. P. Nilsson, *Opuscula Se-
lecta* 2 (Lund, 1952) 52, No. 4, Demeter is represented twice here, in the center and
on the right end of the frieze. This seems unlikely to me. Because the veiled woman
on the right (here pl. 10.1) is grouped with Eumolpos she is perhaps his mother Deiope,
who is represented (with inscription) on a pelike of the Meidias Painter in New York
(37.11.23, from Sicily. Beazley, *ARV*² 1313.7; Graf, *Eleusis* 18, 163–64).

42. Sofia from Apollonia. Metzger 41, No. 39, pl. 23; Graf, *Eleusis* 64–65 (with
convincing interpretation). For Iakchos, who is confused with Eumolpos by Metzger,
Bianchi, and others, see infra nn. 54, 57.

43. No. 03.842. Beazley, *ARV*² 1315.2: Painter of the Karlsruhe Paris; "EleusD" 89,
pl. 20.2; Graf, *Eleusis* 62, n. 17. C. Bérard, *Anodoi* (Rome, 1974) 94, n. 5 doubts the
existence of the inscription, but A. Furtwängler read it: FR 2 (1909) 56–57, n. 3.

44. Brit. Mus. E 140, from Capua. FR pl. 161; Beazley, *ARV*² 459.3; Simon/Hirmer
121, pl. 167; Parke fig. 30.

45. Brussels A 10, from Capua. Beazley, *ARV*² 661.86: Painter of the Yale Lekythos;
Metzger 28, No. 65, pl. 13.2; Bianchi 24, No. 34.

46. Bell-krater Brit. Mus. F 68, from S. Agata dei Goti. Beazley, *ARV*² 1446.1:
Pourtalès Painter; *Recueil Dugas* (supra n. 18) pl. 34.2; Metzger 39, No. 27; Bianchi
24, No. 33; Parke fig. 31. Lekanis lid Tübingen E 183. Beazley, *ARV*² 1477.7: Painter
of Athens 1472; Graf, *Eleusis* 63–64.

47. Plutarch, *Theseus* 33; cf. E. Simon, "Polygnotan Painting and the Niobid Painter,"
AJA 67 (1963) 49.

was dropped later on and all Greek-speaking people were admitted, and finally the Romans also.

In principle, and in contrast to other cults, free people and slaves could be initiated regardless of age or sex. In this respect the Mysteries differed greatly from the other cults of Demeter which we have already discussed. Not only were the Mysteries open to men but the Eleusinian Demeter also had—in contrast to most female deities— men as her chief priests. These peculiarities must be explained by the Mycenaean origin of the Eleusinian Mysteries. They were created, as the Homeric hymn says, in the palace of a king, and this is to be taken literally. As successor of those Eleusinian kings mentioned in the hymn—Triptolemos, Diokles, Eumolpos, Keleos—the archon basileus of Athens superintended the Mysteries, and the two chief priests belonged to clans which claimed descent from heroic kings. Eumolpos is mentioned as basileus in the hymn (473–76); Keryx was thought to be a grandson of king Kekrops.[48] Thus the ties between Athens and Eleusis were strengthened. At a date later than that of the hymn Eumolpos was thought to be of Thracian descent.[49] This is perhaps due to Orphic influence, which cannot be traced in this chapter.[50] In any case, "Thracian" features begin to intrude into Eleusinian iconography after the middle of the fifth century B.C.; one of the earliest vase-paintings to show the hierophant with ependytes is on a stamnos from Eleusis published by Kourouniotes.[51]

The four days of the celebrations in Athens before the great pilgrimage to Eleusis on 19 Boedromion were filled with preparatory rites

48. See supra nn. 26, 40. Hermes was Keryx' father and one of the three daughters of Kekrops (Toepffer, *AG* 81–82) was his mother. She seems to be represented together with her son on the left end of the frieze of the "Regina Vasorum" (supra n. 41).

49. There were two main genealogies. Eumolpos was (a) the son of Poseidon and Chione, the daughter of Boreas and Oreithya, or (b) the son of Mousaios and Deiope (see supra n. 41). In some ancient sources, therefore, two Eumolpoi are differentiated, but they were both "Thracians" and of the same clan: Eumolpos, the son of Mousaios, was the descendant of Eumolpos, the son of Poseidon. See further Richardson, *Hymn* 197–98.

50. See Graf, *Eleusis* passim.

51. Ibid., 636. K. Kourouniotes, "Ἐλευσινιακὴ δᾳδουχία," *ArchEph* 1937, 227–30, pls. 1–4, 9–10; H. Thiersch, *Ependytes und Ephod* (Stuttgart, 1936) pl. 54.1; Beazley, *ARV*² 1052.23: Group of Polygnotos; Metzger 29, No. 68; Bianchi 25, No. 37; Parke fig. 28. The priest with the two torches is usually identified as the *dadouchos*, but two torches seem to be more characteristic of Eumolpos, the ancestor of the hierophants (see supra n. 43), whereas Keryx, the ancestor of the dadouchoi, has only one torch. But perhaps this differentiation was not so strict, because on the Pourtalès krater (supra n. 46) each of them has one torch.

Figures 3 a and b. Eumolpos on skyphos London E 140 and on "Eleusinian pelike" Leningrad St. 1792; see pp. 27–28 and pl. 8.2. After FR pls. 161 and 70 (details).

and offerings. The mystai-to-be had to bathe in the sea for purification. Each of them also had to sacrifice a pig to Demeter. Many votives show the two goddesses or their worshippers with that victim, which is represented in sculpture and on Eleusinian coins.[52]

When the day of the great pilgrimage came, the procession assembled in the morning between the Dipylon and the Sacred Gate in the Kerameikos. From this gate the fourteen-mile-long Sacred Way led to Eleusis.[53] Between the two gates was the Pompeion, a building where processions gathered; the sanctuary of Iakchos, in which this god was venerated along with Demeter and Kore, must have been nearby.[54] His statue was taken out and carried in front of the procession, which arrived at Eleusis towards evening. The participants had crowns of myrtle on their heads and in their hands bundles of leaves, called bakchoi, which were held together with rings.[55] The enthusiastic songs of the mystai, imitated by Aristophanes in his *Frogs* (324ff.), the bundles of leaves, and the statue of Iakchos gave the whole a Dionysiac touch, though from archaic to Roman times the procession is always represented as well ordered.[56]

In studies of Eleusinian iconography the figure of Iakchos has caused great problems because it was confused with the figures of Eumolpos and Keryx, the ancestors of the two noblest Eleusinian clans.[57] Ancient sources and new archaeological material, however, show that Iakchos in Eleusinian representations is no one other than Dionysos. In the official Eleusinian version (schol. Aristophanes, *Frogs* 479) Iakchos is called "Semele's son and giver of wealth," Ploutodotas, who I think is represented with this label on the fragment of a black-figure

52. Mylonas 201; 203; 223, pl. 66; Burkert, *HN* 283–92; Bianchi 27, Nos. 44, 46 (the goddess with *bakchos* and pig is explained as a "youth"—one of the many errors of Bianchi's book).

53. Travlos 302–3, fig. 391. Pompeion: Travlos 477–81; W. Hoepfner et al., *Kerameikos* 10, *Das Pompeion und seine Nachfolgerbauten* (Berlin, 1976).

54. For the Iakcheion see Judeich 364; Graf, *Eleusis* 49–50. For the priest who carried the statue of Iakchos: Maass, *Prohedrie* 119.

55. See J. D. Beazley, "Bakchos Rings," *NumChron* 1941, 1–7.

56. Cf. Deubner pls. 5.2, 6.1. The only representation of mystai in a typically Dionysiac manner on the Niinnion pinax (here pl. 11, infra n. 75) does not show the Mysteries but the Haloa.

57. For them see supra nn. 26, 40. The confusion between Iakchos and Eumolpos began with G. H. Pringsheim, *Archäologische Beiträge zur Geschichte des eleusinischen Kultes* (Munich, 1905); cf. Graf, *Eleusis* 59–65, who has a good treatment of the problem. Graf, ibid., and Richardson, *Hymn* 352, convincingly identify the young man with the ependytes and torches as Eumolpos (or Keryx, see supra n. 51) and not Iakchos.

Attic amphora in the manner of Exekias in Reggio Calabria.[58] Henri Metzger and others have called him Hades-Plouton, but this god never has the epithet Ploutodotas. The beautiful bearded figure stands in front of Demeter's car. There is also Triptolemos (with inscription) crowned with ears of grain and with grain in his left hand, looking to Demeter, who also carries grain. Here he is still the king of the Homeric hymn and not the youth or boy he will be in representations of the fifth and fourth centuries. It is true that the figure I call Iakchos-Ploutodotas is not crowned with ivy and does not carry a *thyrsos*. But the thyrsos, later the most typical attribute of Dionysos, is not pictured as early as Exekias.

In Eleusinian inscriptions the name Dionysos is rare because the Eleusinian name of Dionysos was Iakchos.[59] He sometimes forms a triad with Demeter and Kore. His presence in many Eleusinian pictures has been variously interpreted. Mylonas, for instance, thinks that he was not very important for the Mysteries; others lay stress upon his influence.[60] I think they are right for the following reasons. Characteristic of mystery religions is the identification on the part of the faithful with the grief and joy, and therefore also with the eternal life, of their deity. Accordingly, the Eleusinian mystai during the celebrations on the sixth day of the festival suffered Demeter's afflictions and sorrows after the rape of Kore. In their feelings they even followed her down to the realm of Hades and finally, after the mother and daughter were reunited, they took part in their happiness.[61] To the Greek way of thinking this range of emotions was inspired by Dionysos, the god of ecstasy and enthusiasm. Inspired by this god the mystai could identify themselves with Demeter in her vicissitudes. Thus Iakchos-Dionysos was the mediator between the mystai and the two goddesses. For this reason his statue was carried in front of the procession.

Some scholars have thought that mimes were performed during the sixth day of the Great Mysteries.[62] But the architecture of the Eleusi-

58. No. 4001, from Locri. Beazley, *ABV* 147.6; Metzger 8–9, No. 2, pls. 1.2–2; E. Simon, *Gnomon* 42 (1970) 707 (review of Metzger); Richardson, *Hymn* 319–20; Bianchi 19, No. 12.

59. See Graf, *Eleusis* 65 and passim. Vase paintings with Dionysos in Eleusis: e.g., Metzger pls. 14.1, 15, 17–24.

60. G. Mylonas, "Ἐλευσὶς καὶ Διόνυσος," *ArchEph* 1960, 68–118; Graf, *Eleusis* 51–66.

61. Cf. Simon, *Götter* 102; for Dionysos as god of ecstasy and enthusiasm, ibid. 270.

62. Deubner 84–87; Parke 70: "The 'things done' may have included not merely ritual acts performed by the priests, but also actual mimetic reproduction of some of

nian sanctuary is not suitable for dramatic plays. The "forest" of columns in the Telesterion would have blocked the view. Instead, the mystai heard sounds and voices which inspired their fantasy. So we know of a gong struck by the hierophant, which probably imitated the echo of Kore's cry when Hades seized her.[63] And Eumolpos had his name from singing well. Along with sounds and words, torchlight must have been an essential element of the celebrations,[64] because the two goddesses and the priests often have torches, and the dadouchos is named after the torch. The highlight of the celebrations, the revelation of the Holy Things in the kistai, certainly was illuminated by torches.

We do not know what the kistai contained, but it cannot have been very heavy, because the baskets were carried on the head. In several vase-paintings and in sculpture Demeter is seated on a kiste,[65] but she may also sit on a rectangular chest (the kiste is round) or on other seats.[66] Because the two goddesses in the east pediment of the Parthenon do not sit on kistai but on chests (pl. 10.2) some scholars doubt if they should be identified as Demeter and Kore.[67] But rectangular chests surely served to house the Holy Things when they were not carried in procession. They could not stay in light baskets but had to be shut up. Their place was in the Anaktoron, the Holy of Holies, a little temple in the big Telesterion, into which only the hierophant went. *Anaktoron* means "House of the *(w)anax*," the Mycenaean word for king. The hierophant from the clan of the Eumolpidai took his title from his main task in the Mysteries, the revealing of the Holy Things. He removed them from the kistai, showed them, and brought them back to the Anaktoron. Mylonas thinks that some relics of Mycenaean Eleusis may have survived in the kistai.[68] This is not impossible, but to the crowd of the initiates the Holy Things were surely of symbolical

---

the myths of Demeter. But the climax was the 'things revealed.' These must have been the 'Holy Things' which had just previously been escorted under a veil of secrecy to the Eleusinion in Athens and back."

63. P. Foucart, *Les Mystères d'Éleusis* (Paris, 1914) 34; Simon, *Götter* 102, n. 41.

64. Richardson, *Hymn* 26–28.

65. Metzger 33–36, Nos. 1–14.

66. Square seats of Demeter: Metzger 36–37, Nos. 15–19; to this category also belong Metzger 38–39, Nos. 26–27, although the scholar maintains that Demeter is seated on a low cushion. These documents are Niinnion's pinax (infra, n. 75, here pl. 11) and the Pourtalès krater (supra n. 46, here pl. 8.1).

67. See e.g., Brommer, *Die Skulpturen der Parthenon-Giebel* (Mainz, 1963) 150–52.

68. Mylonas 84–85, 274–75; cf. ibid. 303–4.

rather than historical value, as they assured them of Demeter's care in their lives and thereafter.

With the celebrations in the Telesterion the general initiation was finished. But there was in the hierarchical order of the Mysteries a last step of mystical experience, for which only those who had been initiated in the preceding year were qualified. This was the *Epopteia* ("beholding").[69] A Christian author tells us that in this phase of the Mysteries a fresh-cut ear of grain was shown in silence.[70] This may be true, because grain was Demeter's main symbol and her gift to humanity. Perhaps that event is translated into mythical form in the great Eleusinian relief.[71] The youth Triptolemos, archetype of the mystai, beholds the ears of grain which originally must have been carried by Demeter. He will take them and bring them to mankind, as we know from many vase-paintings and reliefs where he is shown with his miraculous car. But the car is lacking in the great relief, and the action is concentrated in one pregnant moment, the beholding of the grain. This comes very near, I think, to the mystic experience in the Epopteia. The relief seems to have been a kind of altarpiece in the Telesterion and thus would only have been seen by mystai.

HALOA

The last festival which we have to consider is the Haloa.[72] It was celebrated in the winter, on 26 Poseideon. Parke writes: "The name obviously suggested that it was connected with the threshing-floor (ἅλως). . . . but December was not the month for threshing. . . . the name is best left as unexplained." I think an explanation is possible, because the circular assembly area in Delphi, Eleusis, and other Greek sanctuaries was called ἅλως.[73] Furthermore the round threshing floor, which in modern Greece has kept its ancient name, was and is in Greek villages the ideal place for dancing. This fits into the picture of the Haloa which is given us by ancient sources. It was a women's festival and must have been celebrated in earlier times by married women as the Thesmophoria were. But from the fourth century B.C. onwards it was mainly a festival of the *hetairai*. The priests of Eleusis

---

69. Deubner 83; Mylonas 295; Simon, *Götter* 109; Parke 70.
70. Hippolytus, *Phil.* 5.8.39.
71. Simon, *Götter* 113–17.
72. P. Foucart, *BCH* 7 (1883) 514–15; Deubner 60–67; Parke 98–100.
73. Parke 98. See Pomtow, s.v. "Delphoi," *RE* Suppl. 4 (1924) 1296–97.

prepared a banquet in the Telesterion and departed when it began, leaving it to the female symposiasts. They indulged, as Parke comments upon the sources, "in uninhibited obscenity of language," and Deubner has connected some very licentious vase-paintings with the Haloa, for instance hetairai dancing around a big *phallos* symbol.[74] This dance, I think, was performed at the Haloa on the dancing floor, the ἅλως.

While the first part of the festival was restricted to women, later on men were also admitted. This cheerful ending seems to be shown on the pinax of Niinnion, which was a votive to the two Eleusinian goddesses and was found in the sanctuary (pl. 11).[75] It was long thought to be the only representation of the Eleusinian Mysteries, but rather it shows a joyful *komos* of hetairai and their lovers. Nobody carries the bakchos which mystai should certainly have. The komos is led by a priest and a priestess with torches to Demeter and Kore, who sit on chests. In the central figure among the human worshippers of the two goddesses Niinnion herself, who dedicated the pinax, seems to be shown. Because this is a typical hetaira name, the interpretation of the pinax as a picture of the Haloa is corroborated.

I end with a problem. Niinnion and the other hetairai on the pinax carry on their heads dishlike vessels with lids. In my article on this monument I called them *thymiateria*, incense burners, which were used in symposia and also in the cult of Demeter.[76] But Lucy Talcott subsequently wrote to me that she prefers to call these vases *kernoi*, vessels for multiple offerings of grain and other crops which are known from Eleusis, from the Eleusinion in Athens, and from other sanctuaries of the goddess.[77] We know that Demeter was honored by *ker-*

74. Parke 98; Deubner 67, pl. 4.1.

75. Pringsheim (supra n. 57) 52; Farnell 3:24, pl. 16; Deubner 74, pl. 5.1; Nilsson, *GGR* 474, pl. 41.2; Mylonas 213–21, pl. 88, "EleusD" 86–91; H. G. Niemeyer, *Einführung in die Archäologie* (Darmstadt, 1968) 115–16; A. Peschlow-Bindokat (supra n. 18) 105–7; Richardson, *Hymn* 155, 215; Bianchi 24–25, No. 35. In spite of my arguments the last-named authors see on the pinax a representation of the Mysteries. Whereas Peschlow-Bindokat and Bianchi repeat the old error (already disproved by Pringsheim) that the pinax shows two different scenes, Richardson thinks of the *pannychis* after the Iakchos procession and before the day of the celebrations in the Telesterion. But neither bakchoi nor other mystic attributes are shown.

76. A low thymiaterion is shown, e.g., on the frieze Bianchi 26, No. 41, and beside Demeter on the "Regina Vasorum" (supra n. 41, here pl. 10.1); a high thymiaterion appears on a relief lekythos in Paris, Louvre CA 2190 (Metzger 36–37, No. 16, pl. 15).

77. Lucy Talcott's letter is of 16 March 1967. In the meantime the kernoi from Eleusis (cf. Mylonas pl. 87) and from the Eleusinion in Athens (cf. Travlos 201) were

nophoriai, the bringing of kernoi, a kind of thanksgiving offering, but we do not know at what date. Perhaps the kernoi, however, served for incense offerings also. This would be a compromise between the two views.

───────────

studied. In 1977 G. Bakalakis gave a lecture on them in our Institute in Würzburg. The Agora material is published in an article by Jerome J. Pollitt, "Kernoi from the Athenian Agora," *Hesperia* 48 (1979) 205–33.

3

FESTIVALS OF ATHENA, APHRODITE, AND HEPHAISTOS

Apart from the Panathenaia, which we shall consider in the next chapter, the main goddess of Athens, Athena, had many lesser festivals. We shall consider three of them: Chalkeia, Arrephoria, Plynteria. All were celebrations in their own right, but they also contained preparatory rites for the Panathenaia.

CHALKEIA

This festival was celebrated on the last day of Pyanopsion.[1] It was named after the word for copper and bronze, χαλκός, and therefore was a special feast of the bronze-workers. Because Hephaistos was also their patron, this god took part in the festival, too. But the offerings recorded for that day are always for Athena, who as Athena Ergane was the goddess of all handicraft.[2] How dear she was to the Attic potters and vase painters we know from many votive offerings on the Acropolis and from pictures on their vessels. On a hydria of the second quarter of the fifth century B.C. Athena and two Nikai enter a workshop to crown the vase painters.[3] Only a girl sitting on the right end of the frieze is not crowned. A fragment by the Pan Painter from the Acropolis shows men carrying likna (pl. 12.1), perhaps a procession of manual laborers, such as we know from a fragment of Sophokles honoring Athena Ergane.[4] Above all Ergane was the goddess of spinning

1. Deubner 35–36; C. Bérard, (supra n. 13 to chapter 2) 101–14; Parke 38, 92.
2. For Athena Ergane see Bérard (supra n. 13 to chapter 2) 103, n. 25.
3. "Hydria Caputi," Milan, private collection, from Ruvo. J. D. Beazley, "Potter and Painter in Ancient Athens," *ProcBritAc* 30 (1945) passim; J. V. Noble, "The Technique of Attic Vase-Painting," *AJA* 64 (1960) pl. 84; Beazley, *ARV²* 571.73: Leningrad Painter; A. Winter, *Die antike Glanztonkeramik* (Mainz, 1978) 54, pl. 12.
4. *TrGF* 4 (1977) F844 (Radt). This fragment of an unknown Sophoklean drama has

and weaving, an occupation for which she was surely already the patron as the palace goddess of the Mycenaean kings. The Linear B
tablets show that clothing and rugs manufactured in the royal factories
were an important source of wealth.[5] And the great heroines of the
Mycenaean age, like Helen and Penelope, were skillful weavers.

Every fourth year at the Chalkeia, which were celebrated before
the Great Panathenaia, a big loom was set up. Maidens and married
women called Ergastinai ("female workers") began to weave a *peplos*.
It was to be offered to the goddess nine months later at her main
festival, the Great Panathenaia, which took place every fourth year in
the third year of the Olympiad. The weaving required so long a time
because it was complicated: the Gigantomachy, the war between gods
and giants, had to be woven in.

When the work at the loom began, two very young girls in white
garments, the *Arrephoroi*, were present and helped. They were not
much more than seven years old and had been chosen by the archon
basileus from four girls nominated by the Athenian people.[6] Because
of their youth they did not really weave, but it was believed that the
beginning of the work was blessed by their presence. When both of
their parents were alive young boys and girls were called παῖδες
ἀμφιθαλεῖς; they were thought to be dear to the gods, and therefore
they ministered in many cults. To this category the Arrephoroi belonged. They owed their names to another festival, in which they were
the main participants.

ARREPHORIA

This festival was celebrated in midsummer, in the month Skiraphorion, towards the end of the Athenian year;[7] the exact date is not known.

---

already been connected with the Chalkeia procession by Deubner (p. 36). He thought
that the likna mentioned as ritual implements there could only be *kana* (ibid., n. 3).
But the fragment of the Pan Painter (Beazley, *ARV²* 553.31; Bérard [supra n. 1] pl.
26.1, here pl. 12.1) indeed shows likna.

5. *Docs²*: 313–23, 486–89. Sp. Marinatos, "Kleidung," *ArchHom* I:A (1967) 18–21;
Homeric goddesses and heroines weaving: ibid., 1–2.

6. The ancient sources for this election are discussed by Deubner (pp. 10–12; sources
enumerated on p. 11, nn. 6 and 7). Deubner's interpretation of these sources is cor-
rected by W. Burkert, "Kekropidensage und Arrephoria," *Hermes* 94 (1966) 3–4. There
was no "Herbstritus," but only the rite in the month Skiraphorion. The time of the
election is unknown (*contra* Deubner 12 and Burkert, ibid., 5); see infra n. 10.

7. Deubner 9–17; Nilsson, *GGR* 441; Burkert supra n. 6 and *HN* 169–73; Parke
142–43, 159. Deubner calls this festival Arretophoria, "carrying of the unspoken things,"

It was not a feast of the populace but was a secret rite, which is described by our chief source, Pausanias (1.27.3). He speaks of two young girls who "dwell not far from the temple of Polias: the Athenians call them Arrephoroi. These are lodged for a time with the goddess." As we already know, these were the girls chosen by the people and the archon basileus for cult purposes. Like that archon, they changed every year, and for this reason Pausanias speaks of a certain time which they spent on the Acropolis. Their dwelling place there has been excavated and even their playground which, as is known from a literary source, was used for ball games.[8] They lived near the Erechtheion in an area which was the main inhabited area on the Acropolis in Mycenaean times. Pausanias continues: "When the festival comes round they perform the following ceremony by night. They put on their heads the things which the priestess of Athena gives them to carry, but what it is she gives is known neither to her who gives nor to them who carry. Now there is in the city an enclosure not far from the sanctuary of Aphrodite called Aphrodite in the Gardens, and there is a natural underground descent through it. Down this way the maidens go. Below they leave their burdens, and getting something else, which is wrapped up, they bring it back. These maidens are then discharged, and others are brought to the Acropolis in their stead."

This passage was confirmed by the American excavations on the north slope of the Acropolis.[9] Oscar Broneer found the underground way, which was already in use during Late Helladic times, when it had artificial steps. As we know from other Bronze Age citadels like Mycenae and Tiryns, it was a secret way to a well (though the topographical situation is different). In classical times the way led to an open-air precinct of Eros and Aphrodite (fig. 4). This must have been the sanctuary of Aphrodite in the Gardens mentioned by Pausanias. There the nocturnal way of the Arrephoroi ended. They left secret things below to carry other secret things up to the Acropolis.

While Deubner, Parke, and others understand this ritual as a fertility rite which may be compared with the Thesmophoria, Burkert and

---

but most sources, in particular the older ones, have Arrephoria, and the girls who perform the rite are always called Arrephoroi.

8. Travlos 70–71, fig. 91, No. 124. For the Mycenaean dwelling ground on the Acropolis see Sp. Iacovides, Ἡ Μυκηναϊκὴ Ἀκρόπολις τῶν Ἀθηνῶν (Athens, 1962) passim.

9. O. Broneer, "Excavations on the North Slope of the Acropolis in Athens," Hesperia 2 (1933) 329–417; Travlos 55 (bibliography), 72–75, figs. 92–96 (well), 228–32 (sanctuary of Eros and Aphrodite); Parke figs. 58, 59.

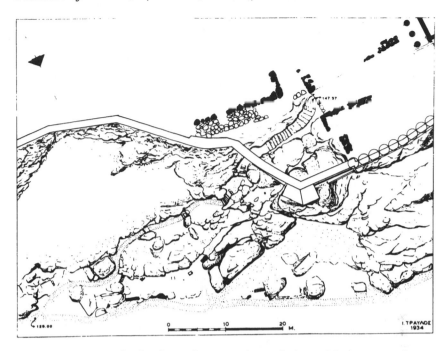

Figure 4. Sanctuary of Aphrodite and Eros on the north slope of the Acropolis, drawing; see p. 40. After Travlos 229, fig. 293.

other modern scholars give a sociological explanation for the festival.[10] As we have seen, this method sometimes works, especially when rites are rooted in the neolithic period. The Arrephoria, however, are not of neolithic but of Mycenaean origin. Burkert, who considers this festival a *rite de passage*, writes: "The routine of the girls' lives as maidens must come to an end. The priestess herself releases them to Eros and Aphrodite under the earth."[11] It must be said, however, that from the practical point of view they did not go under the earth but to an open-air precinct of Aphrodite, from which they returned to the Acropolis. That they were then dismissed can be sufficiently explained according to the Athenian year. It was the last month and soon a new

10. Burkert, *HN* 169–73; also M. Schmidt, "Die Entdeckung des Erichthonios," *AthMitt* 83 (1968) 200–212, especially 203–5. Kron p. 68, on the contrary, is not convinced by Burkert's theory. The first duty of the newly elected Arrephoroi was not at the Chalkeia (contra Burkert, *Hermes* 94 [1966] 4–5) but at the Panathenaia in the first month of the year; see infra p. 67.

11. Burkert, *HN* 171.

archon basileus and two new Arrephoroi were to come. The end of
that year should not be dramatized as Burkert would do with all festivals in the month Skiraphorion. The Athenians, like the Greeks generally before Roman times, did not celebrate a New Year's festival.
They thought rather in greater dimensions of time, namely in the cycle
of four years (the halved μέγας ἐνιαυτός), in which they had their main
festivals, like the Panathenaia or the Olympic games.[12] Finally, the
Arrephoroi were too young to be initiated into the next stage of their
life, marriage. As we know from a passage in Aristophanes' Lysistrata
(641), they were the youngest of all girls who served in Attic sanctuaries, younger than the arktoi of Artemis.[13]

For these reasons Burkert's theory cannot be accepted. The same
must be said about a new theory of Roland Martin and Henri Metzger
which points in a similar direction.[14] They suggest that the Arrephoroi
carried to Aphrodite the balls with which they had played. That this
goddess liked ball games is shown by the fragment of a classical hydria
in Tübingen, on which Aphrodite, identified by an inscription, watches
girls who are playing ball.[15] And it is true that it was a Greek custom
to offer toys to a goddess before a wedding. But Pausanias writes that
the young girls did not understand what they were carrying, and their
balls would have been familiar to them. Because they were only seven
years old, there was no hurry to make offerings of the toys and to rush
into marriage. Thus the interpretation of the festival is still open, and
I am afraid we shall never know what the Arrephoroi carried.

The remark of Pausanias that not even the priestess knew what objects were carried by the Arrephoroi needs explanation. Someone must
have known what they were, and I think this was the archon basileus
as the ritual father of the Arrephoroi. He was the successor of the
Athenian kings, and therefore the Arrephoroi, whom he customarily
chose from the list of the four girls nominated, were his ritual daugh-

12. See supra p. 4.
13. The age of the Arrephoroi may be compared with that of the Vestals in Rome
who were elected by the pontifex maximus when they were between six and ten years
old: C. Koch, s.v. "Vesta," RE 8 A 2 (1958) 1733, 1744. For the arktoi of Artemis see
infra pp. 82–88.
14. R. Martin and H. Metzger, La religion grecque (Paris, 1976) of which I have
seen only the review by N. J. Richardson, JHS 97 (1977) 198.
15. E 112. Corolla Ludwig Curtius (Stuttgart, 1937) pl. 13.3; E. Langlotz, Aphrodite in den Gärten (Heidelberg, 1954) pl. 3.1; Beazley, ARV² 1147.61: Kleophon Painter;
A. Delivorrias, "Das Original der sitzenden 'Aphrodite-Olympias,'" AthMitt 93 (1978)
22, pl. 13.2. For ball-play and Aphrodite generally see A. Kossatz-Deissmann, Dramen des Aischylos auf westgriechischen Vasen (Mainz, 1978) 38–39.

ters.[16] They represented princesses like Pandrosos, Herse, and Aglauros, and they reenacted the duties which the daughters of the royal house had performed for Athena. The fact that in Mycenaean times very small girls served in religious ceremonies is shown, for instance, by the large gold ring from the treasure of Mycenae (pl. 14.1).[17] Here a goddess is sitting beneath a tree. She is visited by two women and attended by two little girls who might be of the same age as the Arrephoroi. One of them, the girl on the left, touches the leaves of the tree, and on the right a Palladion, Athena, appears in the air.

The Arrephoria were a festival not only of Athena but also of Aphrodite in the Gardens because the Arrephoroi connected the sanctuaries of the two goddesses in making their way between one and the other. The meaning of that nocturnal walk can be explained more precisely by an examination of the roles of the participants: Aphrodite in the Gardens, Athena, and the Arrephoroi. The precinct on the north slope was a dependent shrine to the sanctuary of Aphrodite in the Gardens near the Ilissos containing the cult statue by Alkamenes (Pausanias 1.19.2).[18] Another shrine of this kind was at Daphni near the Sacred Way to Eleusis. In Daphni long ago a votive relief was found which shows the type of this goddess (fig. 5). She is leaning against a tree, the branches of which fork behind her head. Angelos Delivorrias has found a fragment of the original cult statue from Daphni which also shows the remains of the tree.[19] He maintains convincingly that this must be similar to Alkamenes' statue near the Ilissos, and that a statue of this type must also have stood on the north slope of the Acropolis. In any case, Aphrodite in the Gardens was connected with a tree or trees, as her epithet suggests.

As we know from Pausanias and other sources she had still another epithet which more closely approached a proper name: Ourania, because she was the oriental Queen of Heaven and the goddess of the morning and the evening star.[20] She was therefore also responsible for

16. See supra n. 6.

17. See supra n. 24 to chapter 2; Simon, *Götter* 181–83, 239–40, fig. 164.

18. Judeich 424; Langlotz (supra n. 15) 36–38, n. 2.

19. A. Delivorrias, "Der Kultstatue der Aphrodite von Daphni," *AntP* 8 (1968) 19–31, pls. 7–9; the votive relief, ibid., 24, fig. 1; H. Schrader, *Phidias* (Frankfurt, 1924) 208, fig. 189. A tree is also represented on the pillar of one statue of this type in the Louvre (not shown in Schrader, ibid., 206). For the attribution of the leaning Aphrodite to Alkamenes see also E. B. Harrison, "Alkamenes' Sculptures for the Hephaisteion: Part II, The Base," *AJA* 81 (1977) 282.

20. W. and H. Gundel, s.v. "Planeten," *RE* 20.2 (1950) 2031–32; H. Gundel, s.v. "Venus (Planet)," *RE* 8 A 1 (1955) 887–91; H. W. Haussig, *Götter und Mythen im*

Figure 5. Votive relief for Aphrodite from Daphni, drawing; see p. 43. After
A. Delivorrias, *AntP* 8 (1968) 24, fig. 1.

the dew, which was believed to be a gift of that planet. Her cult had
arrived in Greece via Cyprus. According to myth Aigeus, the father of
Theseus, had established it in Athens (Pausanias 1.14.7). His purpose
was to promote human fertility, because the royal house was troubled
by the lack of children. Aphrodite in the Gardens, therefore, was connected not only with trees and the dew but also with human fertility.
How do the functions of this goddess tally with the rite of the Arrephoria?

It has been argued that in Skiraphorion, the month of the grain
harvest, fertility rites are out of place. The festival could not have

Vorderen Orient (Stuttgart, 1965) 85–86. For the planet Venus and the dew see E.
Simon, "Zur Augustusstatue von Prima Porta," *RömMitt* 64 (1957) 56. To J. Russo, of
Haverford College I owe the knowledge of Deborah D. Boedeker's *Aphrodite's Entry
into the Greek Epic, Mnemosyne* Suppl. 32 (Leiden, 1974) where the name of the
goddess is connected with dew.

been celebrated to fertilize the grain-growing soil. But there were other crops, especially the most Attic of all, the olive. The prizes at the Great Panathenaia were amphoras filled with olive oil from trees belonging to the state.[21] They all were thought to have sprung from the sacred olive tree on the Acropolis, Athena's gift to Athens. The months following Skiraphorion are crucial for the olive crop, which is gathered in later fall and in winter. If there is not enough dew the fruit remains small. Deubner suggested that the Arrephoria might have been connected with dew for the olive tree on the Acropolis.[22] Although Deubner had made the correct assumption, he did so despite the fact that he did not take Aphrodite's participation in the rite into consideration. When the presence of the garden goddess is taken into account, Deubner's theory is actually strengthened, and it is finally placed beyond doubt by the following arguments.

Athena's olive tree stood near the Erechtheion in the Pandroseion, an open-air sanctuary of Pandrosos, who was named for dew. Pandrosos in the myth had a sister, Herse, a name which also means dew, and sometimes in modern literature they are called dew-sisters. Both were daughters of King Kekrops, along with a third sister, Aglauros.[23] Athena gave to them the basket in which the newborn Erichthonios was hidden, and forbade them to open it. Disobeying Athena, two of them lifted the lid, were frightened by a demoniacal snake, and hurled themselves from the Acropolis. To Pandrosos, who (in most versions) had remained faithful, Athena entrusted a part of her precinct and the care of the olive tree. There is full agreement among scholars that this is the *aition* for the rite of the Arrephoroi, who were not allowed to see the contents of what they carried. The story may have been told as a warning to the little girls not to be curious. Moreover, there seems to have been a tragedy in the fate of Kekrops' daughters, as is shown by the picture on an ornate Apulian calyx-krater in Malibu (pls. 12.2, 13).[24] In the center Pandrosos sits on a large altar with the basket on

21. See infra n. 3 to chapter 4; for the olive trees of Attica see also Richter (n. 20 to chapter 2) 137.

22. Deubner 14: "Es muss sich um einen Ritus handeln, der reichlichen Tau, namentlich in der heissen Jahreszeit, sichern sollte. Dieser Ritus galt höchstwahrscheinlich dem heiligen Ölbaum, der ja im Bezirk der Pandrosos stand."

23. Aglauros or Agraulos was also the name of their mother; the three sisters, therefore, were also called Agraulids. For their myth and the representations in Attic art see Kron 67–72; E. B. Harrison (supra n. 19) 270–84. In cult they did not represent a triad but were venerated separately, see, e.g., R. Hanslik, s.v. "Pandrosos," *RE* 18.3 (1949) 553–59.

24. J. Paul Getty Museum. Cf. *RVAp* I:440, No. 22a. "The vase is by the Black Fury Painter: *RVAp* I: chapter 7, pp. 165ff. Cf. especially the Malibu oinochoe p. 167.12"

her lap. Her sisters are driven away by Athena and are about to hurl themselves from the Acropolis. On the left are Kekrops, his son Erysichthon, and, perhaps, Hermes. Near the altar stands an olive tree. Because this tree is part of the etiological myth, it must be connected with the Arrephoria, too. Like the royal forerunners of the Arrephoroi, it came from Mycenaean times when the cult of trees was in high esteem.

In fact, therefore, the rite performed by the Arrephoroi was a fertility charm. Its purpose was the magic strengthening of the olive trees and, at the same time, the life force of Athens and her people, miraculously represented in the sacred olive on the Acropolis: Herodotus tells us that immediately after the sack of Athens by the Persians the burnt tree put forth a new shoot (8.55). The little Arrephoroi, therefore, successors of the dew-sisters, had a very important, time-honored task.

PLYNTERIA

Two months before the Panathenaia, in the last week of Thargelion, were celebrated the Plynteria, the feast of the bath, a common Ionian festival.[25] On that day the cult statue of Athena Polias was washed in the sea. A short time previously, on a day called *Kallynteria,* her temple had been cleaned. Thus the newly washed image came back into a clean house. The day of the Plynteria was inauspicious because on it Athena Polias left Athens to bathe near Phaleron. The Romans, who had many more days of this character, would have called it a *dies nefastus*.

The cult statue was a (probably) seated Athena without weapons. It

---

(A. Cambitoglou in a letter of 1 June 1979). J. Frel kindly allowed me to study the original (of which Trendall saw only a fragment) and gave me the photographs reproduced here (pls. 12.2, 13). Many details were in white paint, which is not well preserved. For example, the whole altar was painted white; it resembled in color, size, and shape the altar on which Orestes sits on the volute-krater of the Ilioupersis Painter in Naples 3223. See A. D. Trendall and T. B. L. Webster, *Illustrations of Greek Drama* (London, 1971) III:3.28. Kekrops is shown in purely human shape (cf. Kron 97–103). His son Erysichthon (both legs are restored) is a youth fighting with a big snake. Because this snake was painted white, it is not well preserved; but its head and other details are incised. This must be the snake from the basket of Erichthonios. Of the figure above the left handle, only the legs (with boots) are preserved. Because Hermes was connected with Kekrops' daughters (see Kron 94–95), he is perhaps represented here.

25. Deubner 17–22; L. Ziehen, s.v. "Plynteria," *RE* 21.1 (1951) 1060–65; Parke 152–55; ibid., about the Kallynteria. Plynteria celebrated throughout Ionia: Nilsson, *GF* 469.

Figure 6. Seated Athena, terracotta, from the Acropolis, drawing. Berlin (east); see p. 48. After F. Winter, *Die Typen der figürlichen Terrakotten* I (1903) 48, fig. 2.

was carved of olive wood and wore real clothes and jewelry: the head was adorned with a high *stephane* (crown) of gold.[26] We know its appearance from inscriptions on black-figure vases and from a large series of late archaic terracottas found on the Acropolis. Some of them

26. On the type of Athena Polias: A. Frickenhaus, "Das Athenabild des Alten Tempels in Athen," *AthMitt* 33 (1908) 17–32; C. J. Herington, *Athena Parthenos and Athena Polias* (Manchester, 1955) passim. I follow Frickenhaus because of the large series of terracottas from the Acropolis, which show a seated Athena; cf. Simon, *Götter* 194, fig. 177 = E. Rohde, *Griechische Terrakotten* (Tübingen, 1968) pl. 12. The scholion to Demosthenes *c. Androt.* 13 speaks of three statues of Athena on the Acropolis, but

have a *gorgoneion* painted on the breast and thus the interpretation is certain (fig. 6).

Women of the Attic clan Praxiergidai disrobed the goddess in the temple.[27] The statue was then wrapped up and taken to Phaleron in a procession. It was accompanied by mounted Athenian ephebes, who also, as we have seen, escorted the Holy Things from Eleusis to Athens. The Plynteria procession had something of a mystery, too. With the exception of the Praxiergidai, who in the evening clothed the returning goddess with a clean peplos, and the two girls, the λουτρίδες who washed her, nobody was allowed to see her unclothed.

The bathing of cult images—male and female—was an old custom in many sanctuaries in Greece and elsewhere.[28] In Athens specifically we know of one other goddess—Aphrodite—who had a bathing festival. It was probably called the Aphrodisia.

APHRODISIA

This festival was celebrated not for Aphrodite in the Gardens, who took part in the Arrephoria, but for Aphrodite Pandemos, who had her sanctuary on the southwestern slope of the Acropolis.[29] Pausanias mentions it between the Asklepieion and the Propylaia (1.22.3). The visitor of today can see there architectural remains of early Hellenistic times. They can be identified with the sanctuary of Pandemos by the inscription and frieze. The ornaments are doves, the holy birds of the goddess, which carry knotted woolen fillets in their beaks (pl. 15.1). With these fragments Luigi Beschi reconstructed the *aedicula* of Aphrodite Pandemos and showed its proper place (fig. 7).

We know about the cult from an inscription of the year 287/86 B.C., which prescribes the rites connected with Aphrodite's festival.[30] The sanctuary was purified with the blood of a dove, the altars were anointed, and the cult images were conducted in procession to the

differentiates them only by their material—olive wood, bronze and ivory with gold: Overbeck, *SQ* No. 642. *Stephane* and other jewelry: *IG* II² 1424a, lines 362ff.

27. Toepffer, *AG* 133–36; Sokolowski, *LS* No. 15.

28. Cf. Nilsson, *GF* 48 (Hera in Samos), 255–56 (Artemis and Athena in Ankyra); Tacitus *Germania* 40 (I owe this reference to C. Stephen Jaeger of Bryn Mawr College). For the bathing of the statue of a Hittite god see K. Bittel, *Hattusha* (New York and Oxford, 1970) 13.

29. Deubner 215–16; Bömer, "Pompa" 1914. The sanctuary: Judeich 285; L. Beschi, "Contributi di Topografia Ateniese," *ASAtene* 45/46 (1967/1968) 520–26; "Pandemos" 11. For the name Aphrodisia see Deubner 216.

30. *IG* II² 659; Sokolowski *LS* No. 39; Beschi (supra n. 29) 525, but read in 1. 16: "decreto del 287/86 (*IG* II² 659)".

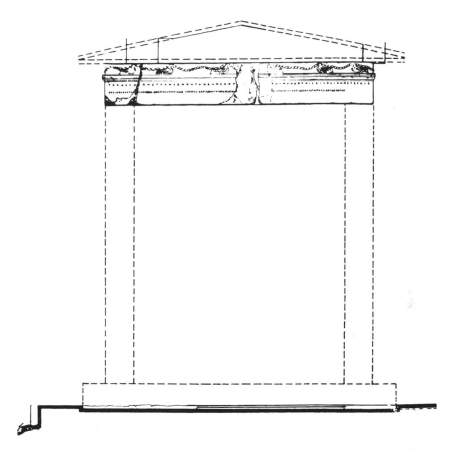

Figure 7. Reconstruction of the aedicula of Aphrodite Pandemos; see p. 48. After L. Beschi, *ASAtene* 45/46 (1967/68) 524, fig. 9.

place where they were washed. There were two of them because Aphrodite Pandemos was venerated along with the goddess Peitho ("Persuasion"). This whole ritual had to be performed, as the inscription tells, κατὰ τὰ πάτρια ("as it had been in times of old").

The procession in honor of Aphrodite and Peitho probably took place shortly after the beginning of the Attic year, on 4 Hekatombaion. The fourth of each month was a holy day of Aphrodite.[31] Parke does not discuss this festival, though it is well attested by the inscription mentioned above. Pausanias writes: "The worship of Vulgar Aphrodite and

31. Deubner 215, n. 4 (the inscription found by Broneer also in Travlos 230); Parke 21. For the *tetradistai* see also Poland, s.v. "Τετραδισταί," *RE* 5 A 1 (1934) 1070–71.

of Persuasion was instituted by Theseus when he gathered the Athenians from the townships into a single city. In my time the ancient images were gone, but the existing images were made by no obscure artists" (1.22.3). This is not the only evidence for the important role which Aphrodite had played in the *synoikismos*, the political unification of Attica ascribed to Theseus.[32] According to these and other sources her epithet Pandemos is to be understood as "the common Aphrodite of the united Attic people."

It is true that the festival Synoikia, which celebrated the unification of Attica, is mentioned in the ancient sources among the festivals of Athena.[33] It took place in the same month, Hekatombaion, between the Aphrodisia and the Panathenaia. But we know from Plutarch's life of Theseus that Aphrodite was a special patroness of this hero. And we know from other sources that Aphrodite's companion Peitho was a helper not only in affairs of love but also in politics. Not only in Athens but also in Argos Peitho had helped to form the first civic community. Her cult in Paros is already attested in the seventh century B.C., when it was carried to Thasos.[34] As I have shown elsewhere, Athenian coins of the late archaic period, triobols and smaller coins, have on one side Athena and on the other the popular Aphrodite Pandemos, the goddess who belonged "to the unified people."[35]

I cite these archaic examples because otherwise one could think that Pandemos and Peitho belonged to a relatively late stratum of Attic cults, since they are omnipresent in vase-paintings of the rich style.[36] One need think only of the Eretria Painter's epinetron, on which Aphrodite and Peitho, both with inscriptions, are seated and served by girls and Erotes.[37] The painter may have thought of the cult images on the southwestern slope and may have rendered them in a free manner. But Aphrodite and Peitho had been mighty goddesses earlier, for instance in the tragedies of Aischylos, where their might is a matter more of political than of erotic power.[38] Towards the end of the *Oresteia* Athena twice invokes Peitho in the crucial situation when she finally succeeds in persuading the Erinyes (*Eum.* 885ff. and 970ff.).

32. "Pandemos" 11–12; the two most important sources are Apollodoros of Athens (second century B.C.), *FGrHist* 244 F 113, and Pausanias 1.22.3.

33. Deubner 36–38; Parke 31–32.

34. For Peitho in Argos, Paros and Thasos see E. Simon, s.v. "Peitho," *EAA* 6 (1965) 6.

35. "Pandemos" 5–18, pl. 1.2.

36. See Hamdorf (supra n. 8 to Introduction) 64.

37. Beazley, *ARV*² 1250.34; Simon/Hirmer pl. 216.

38. "Pandemos" 13–14.

In Plato's *Symposion* Aphrodite Pandemos is contrasted with Aphrodite Ourania. This is a sophistic differentiation, and the speaker of this passage is in fact a sophist. Nevertheless, the definition of the two goddesses, in which Pandemos appears morally inferior to Ourania, has ever since been looked upon as Platonic; it had a strong influence on Neoplatonism and on Renaissance thought and art.[39] This, however, has nothing to do with the ancient Attic cult, in which Ourania and Pandemos were not morally differentiated. Both of them were manifestations of the great oriental goddess whose way from Ascalon via Cyprus to Greece is described in Herodotus (1.105). In the Orient she was a goddess of love and war and a tutelary goddess of cities. She was invoked as Inanna Ishtar, Queen of Heaven, and by other names.[40] She often wore weapons, which she retained also in some of her Greek sanctuaries, although not in Athens. To speak in Greek terms, she was a kind of mixture of Aphrodite and Athena, but after Homer had defined each of these two goddesses clearly and very differently, they could no longer be confused. In certain ancient cults, however, as in the temple at Gortyn in Crete, they were closely connected or even identical.[41]

In Athens, Aphrodite had two sanctuaries on the slopes of Athena's citadel, the Acropolis. As we have seen, one of them, Aphrodite in the Gardens, played an important part in the Arrephoria, and the other had a festival of bathing like Athena's Plynteria. In the above-mentioned early Hellenistic inscription, Pandemos and Peitho are venerable goddesses with an old cult. They had a state festival because they belonged to the unified people of Attica.

FESTIVALS OF HEPHAISTOS

Hephaistos was one of the main deities of Athens.[42] At the beginning of Aischylos' *Eumenides* the Pythia calls the Athenians "children of Hephaistos" (13). He was the father of King Erechtheus, of whom Homer says (*Il.* 2.547–51 in Lattimore's translation):

> . . . Erechtheus, whom once Athene
> Zeus' daughter tended after the grain-giving fields had born him,

---

39. See especially E. Panofsky, *Studies in Iconology* (New York, 1939) passim.
40. Haussig (supra n. 20) 81–89.
41. *Gortyn* I (Rome, 1968) 249–50; R. Hampe, *Kretische Löwenschale des siebten Jahrhunderts v. Chr.* (Heidelberg, 1969) 37 with n. 104; "Pandemos" 13.
42. Simon, *Götter* 215–28; F. Brommer, *Hephaistos* (Mainz, 1978) passim.

and established him to be in Athens in her own rich temple;
there as the circling years go by the sons of the Athenians
make propitiation with rams and bulls sacrificed.

Uta Kron has shown convincingly that here Homer indicates an offering for Erechtheus and not for Athena.[43] It must have been an Athenian festival because the phrase "as the circling years go by" is used in
Homer for festivals which return every year or after several years.

It is a pity that we do not know more about this ancient festival of
Erechtheus. The same can be said about the celebrations in honor of
Hephaistos, the father of this king (also called Erichthonios).[44] Homer
does not even mention his fatherhood because he did not like the
myth of the god's unrequited love for Athena, who nevertheless nursed
his earthborn son. We have discussed his basket in the etiological myth
of Kekrops' daughters, who opened the lid.[45] On a calyx-krater of the
rich style in Schloss Fasanerie near Fulda the basket of Erichthonios
stands next to the sacred olive tree of the Acropolis (pl. 14.2).[46] It is
depicted as closed and covered by a cult rug. Old King Kekrops, whose
hair was painted white, and Athena bring offerings to the newborn
child. Both are ministered to by Nike. Also there is Poseidon, who
rests on a *kline*, and on the left Zeus sits on a throne. Brommer and
Kron have shown that the deities represented there were all venerated in the Erechtheion, the "house of Erechtheus," whose basket is
the center of the composition. Can the two little girls between Poseidon and Zeus be identified as Arrephoroi?[47] I do not think so, because
their mythical forerunners, the daughters of Kekrops, are shown above
the left handle. The two girls are perhaps Kosmo and Trapezo, as two
priestesses of Athena were called.[48] They took their names from *kos-
mos*, "decoration" and from *trapeza*, "dining table," which fit into the
context of the vase-painting. Above the right handle Hephaistos, seen
from the back, rests on a mattress.[49] He is not identified by inscrip-

43. Kron 32–37; cf. Melldahl/Flemberg 77.
44. For the identity of Erechtheus and Erichthonios see Kron 37–39. Representations of the birth of Erichthonios with Hephaistos: Kron 55–64; E. B. Harrison (supra
n. 19) 280–84.
45. See supra n. 24.
46. *CVA* Deutschland 11, Schloss Fasanerie 1 (Munich, 1956) pls. 46–48; Beazley,
*ARV*² 1346.1: Kekrops Painter; Kron 61–63, pl. 5.1.
47. So I have tried to call them in Simon/Hirmer 153, but this is questionable. E. B.
Harrison (supra n. 19) 273 names one of the girls "perhaps Hebe."
48. Lykourgos F 48 (Blass); Toepffer, *AG* 122. This is a competent source because
the author himself was of the Eteoboutadai: Davies *APF* 348–53.
49. He is shown without a beard. This youthful appearance is known from other
representations on vases of the rich style (e.g., J. D. Beazley, "Excavations at Al Mina,

tions, which are totally lacking on the krater, but by the pair of tongs which he holds. Above him an Eros hovers and pours wine into his phiale. From the other side Hermes comes with some message, pointing to the central group. We know of a festival Deipnophoria, the "bringing of food," which was celebrated for the daughters of Kekrops.[50] The festival for the inhabitants of the Erechtheion which is represented on this calyx-krater could be called Deipnophoria, too. Hephaistos takes part in it, but he also had a festival of his own, the Hephaisteia, of which we do not know the exact date.[51] Parke lists it under festivals which are not localized in the calendar.

The main source is an inscription from the year 421/20 B.C. which contains a reorganization of the cult but is unfortunately only a fragment.[52] The main features of the festival were dithyrambic choruses and a torch-race, along with a procession and the offering of many cattle in the Hephaisteion. The torch-race ($\lambda\alpha\mu\pi\alpha\delta\epsilon\delta\rho\omega\mu\acute{\iota}\alpha$), was meaningful in the cult of Hephaistos, who was connected with fire. Deubner has shown that this race existed long before the time of the inscription mentioned above.[53] Torch-races also occur frequently on Attic vases of the fifth and the early fourth century.[54] But not all pictures can be related to the Hephaisteia. There were also, as we shall see, the races at the Panathenaia (pl. 22.2), as well as the races at the Prometheia in honor of Prometheus, who had stolen fire from heaven.[55] After the Persian wars torch-races were instituted for Pan, who had helped the Athenians at Marathon.[56] Finally, the Thracian goddess Bendis was honored with horse-races with torches, as is well known from the beginning of Plato's *Republic*. Torch-races were common Attic themes, in reality and in art. It is therefore difficult to interpret such races in vase-painting as belonging to a certain cult. Heide Froning, however, succeeded in showing that on the big volute-krater by

---

Sueidia. III. The Red-figured Vases," *JHS* 59 [1939] 30–32) but also from the early classical white ground cup in London D4. Beazley, *ARV*[2] 869.55: Tarquinia Painter.

50. Philochoros, *FGrHist* 328 F 183, with Jacoby's commentary; cf. Deubner 14, n. 8; Ferguson 21.

51. Deubner 212–13; Parke 171–72; E. B. Harrison, "Alkamenes' Sculptures for the Hephaisteion: Part III, Iconography and Style," *AJA* 81 (1977) 414–16.

52. *IG* I[2] 84; Sokolowski, *LS* No. 13; for the interpretation see Deubner and Harrison (supra n. 51); also Froning 78–81, 84, 87.

53. Deubner 212–13.

54. Froning 78–81, 96, 118–19.

55. Deubner 211–12; Parke 171–72.

56. Deubner 213; E. Simon, "Ein nordattischer Pan," *AntK* 19 (1976) 19–23; Parke 172–73.

Polion in Ferrara a torch-race at the Hephaisteia is represented.[57] It proceeds around the neck of the vase (pl. 15.2), whereas the main pictures can be connected with the themes of dithyrambic choruses at that festival.

Perhaps the calendar-frieze can help us to place the Hephaisteia within the Athenian year. In the month Mounychion, to the right of one of the Byzantine crosses, a naked man is running with a torch (pl. 2.1). He is rightly called by Deubner the personification of summer.[58] But why is he carved moving like a torch-bearer? Perhaps because he has some relationship to one of the many Attic torch-race festivals. This cannot be to the races at the Panathenaia, Bendideia, or Paneia, which took place in other months, not in Mounychion. There remain only the Hephaisteia and the Prometheia.[59] As Hephaistos was the more important for the Athenians, I conclude that his festival must be placed in Mounychion, at the beginning of summer.

57. T. 127. Beazley, ARV² 1171.1; Froning 78–81, pl. 14.2. For Bendis see Bömer, "Pompa" 1929–30.

58. Deubner 252; he thought the figure holds ears of grain.

59. E. B. Harrison (supra n. 51) places the Hephaisteia near the time of the Chalkeia (pp. 415–16), but her arguments are not compelling.

1 and 2. Calendar-frieze, Athens, Little Metropolis; see pp. 6–7, 77, 81, 83, 90. Photo, Deutsches Archäologisches Institut Athen.

Plate 1

1–3. Calendar-frieze. Elaphebolion to Boedromion, Athens, Little Metropolis; see pp. 6–8, 16, 25, 54, 59, 81, 102. Photo, Deutsches Archäologisches Institut Athen.

Plate 2

1–3. Calendar-frieze. Pyanopsion to Gamelion, Athens, Little Metropolis; see pp. 6, 7, 14, 16, 18, 21, 77, 83, 90, 100, 101. Photo, Deutsches Archäologisches Institut Athen.

Plate 3

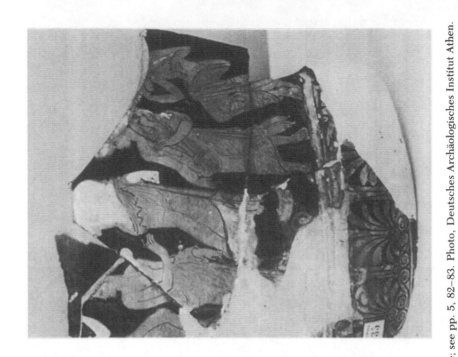

1 and 2. Calyx-krater. Athenian months, Athens, Nat. Mus. from Hermione: see pp. 5, 82–83. Photo, Deutsches Archäologisches Institut Athen.

Plate 4

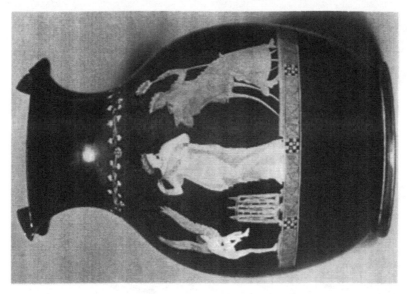

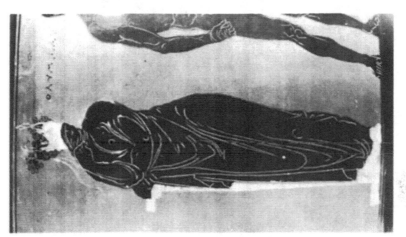

1. Panathenaic amphora. Personification of the Olympiad, Harvard 1925.30.124, Hoppin bequest; see p. 5. Photo, Fogg Art Museum, Harvard University.

2. Oinochoe (chous). Dionysos and Pompe, New York, Met. Mus. 25.190; see pp. 6, 70, 96. Photo, Metropolitan Museum of Art.

Plate 5

1–3. Oinochoe. Dipolieia, Munich J 1335; see pp. 10, 74n.9. Photo, Staatliche Antikensammlungen München (C. H. Krüger-Moessner).

Plate 6

1. Cup. Bouzyges plowing, London, Brit. Mus. 1906.12–15.1; see p. 21. Photo, British Museum.

2. Bell-krater. Bouzyges plowing, Harvard 60.345, from Vari; see p. 21. Photo, Fogg Art Museum, Harvard University.

Plate 7

1. Bell-krater. Eleusinian scene. London, Brit. Mus. F 68, from S. Agata dei Goti; see pp. 28, 34n.66, 58. Photo, British Museum.

2. "Eleusinian pelike." Leningrad St. 1792, from Kerch; see pp. 27, 27n.39, 28, 58. Photo, Hermitage Leningrad.

Plate 8

Hydria. Eleusinian goddesses, Abegg-Stiftung Bern; see p. 27. Photo, Abegg-Stiftung Bern.

Plate 9

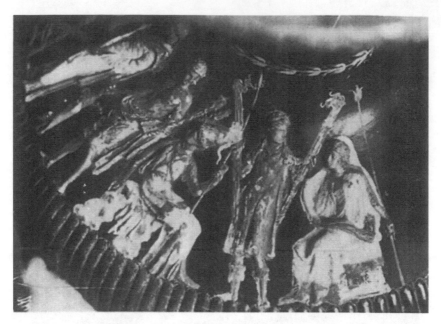

1. "Regina Vasorum." Eleusinian scene, Leningrad 51659, from Cumae; see pp. 28, 28n.41, 36n,76. Photo, Hermitage Leningrad.

2. East pediment of the Parthenon. Eleusinian goddesses, London, Brit. Mus.; see p. 34. Photo, British Museum.

Plate 10

Pinax of Niinnion. Athens, Nat. Mus. 11036, from Eleusis; see pp. 32n.56, 34n.66, 36.
Photo, Alinari 24335.

Plate 11

1. Fragment of an amphora of special shape. Procession for Athena Ergane, Athens, Nat. Mus. Acr. 618; see pp. 38, 39n.4. Photo, Deutsches Archäologisches Institut Athen.

2. Apulian calyx-krater. Athena and the daughters of Kekrops, Malibu, J. Paul Getty Mus.; see pp. 45, 46, 46n.24. Photo, The J. Paul Getty Museum.

Plate 12

Apulian calyx–krater. See pl. 12.2.

Plate 13

1. Gold ring. Athens, Nat. Mus. from Mycenae; see pp. 23n.24, 43. Photo, Hirmer Photoarchiv München Nr. 584.3037.

2. Calyx-krater. Athena and Kekrops, Schloss Fasanerie (Fulda); see p. 52. Photo, Schloss Fasanerie.

Plate 14

1. Sanctuary of·Aphrodite Pandemos. Athens; see p. 48. Photo, author.

2. Volute-krater, neck. Torch-race for Hephaistos; Ferrara, from Spina T. 127; see p. 54. Photo, Soprintendenza alle antichità, Bologna.

Plate 15

1. Hydria. Uppsala, University 352; see p. 61. Photo, Uppsala University.

2. Band-cup. Offering to Athena, private collection; see p. 63. Photo, D. Widmer, Basel.

Plate 16

1. "Panathenaic" hydria. Florence, private collection; see p. 64. Photo, D. Lohmann, Essen.

2. Band-cup. See pl. 16.2

Plate 17

After Th. Bowie and D. Thimme, *The Carrey Drawings of the Parthenon Sculptures* (Bloomington, 1971). 1. Carrey's drawing of the north frieze of the Parthenon, slabs IV–VI. Paris, Bibliothèque Nationale; see pp. 64–65.

2. Carrey's drawing of the north frieze, slabs VII and VIII; see pl. 18.1 and pp. 62–63, 65.

3. Carrey's drawing of the south frieze, slabs XXXV–XXXVII; see pl. 18.1 and pp. 62, 65.

Plate 18

1. Hydriaphoroi from the north frieze of the Parthenon. Athens, Acropolis Museum; see pp. 60, 63, 64. Photo, Hirmer Photoarchiv München No. 654.1951.

2. Officials from the north frieze of the Parthenon. Athens, Acropolis Museum; see p. 62. After F. Brommer, *Der Parthenonfries* (Mainz, 1977) pl. 64.

Plate 19

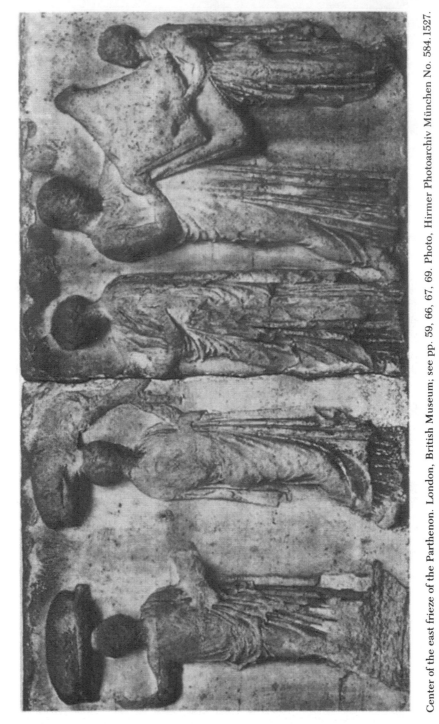

Center of the east frieze of the Parthenon. London, British Museum; see pp. 59, 66, 67, 69. Photo, Hirmer Photoarchiv München No. 584.1527.

Plate 20

Parthenon, west frieze. Athens; see pp. 59, 70. Photo, author.

Plate 21

1. Marshals and girls from the right half of the east frieze of the Parthenon. Paris, Louvre; see pp. 60, 69. Photo, Hirmer Photoarchiv München No. 561.1042.

2. Bell-krater. Lampadedromia, Harvard 1960.344, bequest D. M. Robinson; see pp. 53, 64.

Plate 22

1. Volute-krater. Apollo Pythios, Ferrara, from Spina T. 57 C VP; see p. 79. Photo, Hirmer Photoarchiv München No. 581.1406.

2. Bell-krater. Dithyrambic victory, Copenhagen Chr. VIII 939; see p. 23. After *CVA* Copenhagen 4 pl. 147.

Plate 23

2. Krateriskos. Brauron; see p. 83. Photo, Brauron excavations.

1. Votive relief. Artemis Elaphebolos, Cassel; see pp. 81, 81n.41. Photo, Staatliche Kunstsammlungen Kassel.

Plate 24

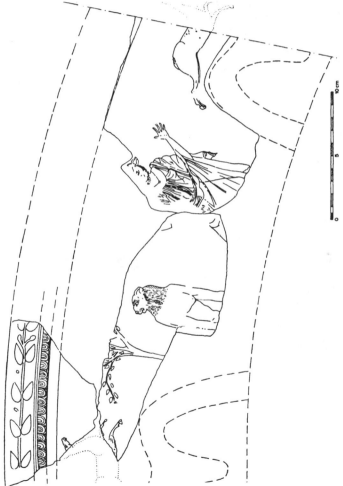

1 and 2. Drawing and photograph of krateriskos. Private collection; see p. 87. After *AntK* 20 (1977) 98, fig. C and photograph by the owner.

Plate 25

Amphora. Dionysos Oschophoros, Munich 2344; see p. 90. Photo, Hirmer Photoarchiv München No. AM 2344/2.

Plate 26

Calyx-krater. Dionysos and Apollo shaking hands in Delphi, Leningrad St. 1807, from Kerch; see p. 90. Photo, Hermitage Leningrad.

Plate 27

1 and 2. Oinochoe (chous). Victor and Nike, Würzburg H 4937; see p. 95. Photo, Martin-von-Wagner-Museum (Karl Öhrlein).

3. Oinochoe (chous). Satyr on mule, Würzburg H 5387; see p. 96. Photo, Martin-von-Wagner-Museum (Karl Öhrlein).

Plate 28

Bell-krater. Dithyrambic chorus, Copenhagen 13817; see p. 98. Photo, National Museum Copenhagen.

Plate 29

1. Skyphos. Satyr and basilinna, private collection; see p. 97. Photo, D. Widmer, Basel.

2. Skyphos. Aiora, Berlin (east) 2589, from Chiusi; see p. 99. After J. Charbonneaux, R. Martin, and F. Villard, *La Grèce Classique* (Paris, 1969) 254 fig. 288.

Plate 30

1. Calyx-krater. Dionysos and basilinna, Tarquinia RC 4197, from Tarquinia; see p. 97. Photo, Alinari 26041 (right).

2. Chous. Aiora, Athens, private collection; see p. 99. Photo, Deutsches Archäologisches Institut Athen.

Plate 31

1. Terracotta-mask of Dionysos.
Heidelberg TK 61, from Boeotia; see p. 103. Photo, Archäologisches Institut der Universität
Heidelberg (H. Wagner).

2. Cup. Lenaia, Berlin (west) F 2290; see p. 100.
Photo, Antikenmuseum Staatliche Museen Preus-
sischer Kulturbesitz (I. Geske).

3. Column-krater. Early tragedy, Basel, Antikenmuseum BS 415; see p. 103. Photo,
Antikenmuseum Basel.

Plate 32

4

PANATHENAIA AND PARTHENON

The Panathenaia are better known to us than any other Greek festival.[1] The day of the Panathenaic procession was 28 Hekatombaion, Athena's birthday, when she had sprung from the head of Zeus (Kallisthenes, *FGrHist* 124 F 52). This myth was represented in the east pediment of the Parthenon. The birthday of the main goddess must have been an old Athenian festival by the time it was reorganized in Peisistratid Athens. The name of the month Hekatombaion seems to be connected with the *hekatombai*, offerings of a hundred cows, to Athena. Some ancient and modern authors derived it from a hypothetical *hekatombe* to Apollo[2] but it is perhaps better explained by the many cattle offered at the Panathenaia.

There is plenty of archaeological evidence for this festival. One may recall the Panathenaic prize amphoras (figs. 8a–b),[3] or archaic Attic coins on which such amphoras are an emblem,[4] or classical vases showing special Panathenaic competitions, for instance young horsemen throwing a spear at a shield.[5] This event is also mentioned in the long inscriptional catalogue of Panathenaic prizes of the early fourth century, which is one of our chief sources (*IG* II² 2311). It was found on the Acropolis, as were archaic inscriptions concerning the Panathenaia;[6] among these there are even fragments of the inscription record-

1. Deubner 22–35; Ziehen 457–89 (additions: Bömer, "Pompa" 1928); Burkert, *HN* 173–77; Parke 33–50.

2. *Etym. Magn.* 321.5; Parke 29; see, however, Deubner 201: "Der gleiche Festname [scil. Hekatombaia] kommt auch sonst vor, ohne dass Apollo überall der Herr des Festes gewesen wäre." Thus the festival of Hera in Argos had the name Hekatombaia (Nilsson, *GF* 43).

3. Beazley (supra n. 8 to Introduction) 88–100; J. Frel, *Panathenaic Prize Amphoras*, Kerameikos 2 (Athens, 1973).

4. P. R. Franke and M. Hirmer, *Die griechische Münze* (Munich, 1964) pl. 114 above, left.

5. Beazley, "Panathenaia," *AJA* 47 (1943) 441–65; B. A. Sparkes, "Quintain and the Talcott Class," *AntK* 20 (1977) 8–25.

6. A. Raubitschek, *Dedications from the Athenian Akropolis* (Cambridge, Mass.,

Figures 8 a and b. Panathenaic prize amphoras; see p. 55. a. Carlsruhe, Badisches Landesmuseum 65.45, attributed to Exekias. Beazley, *Paralipomena* 61.8 bis. Photo, Badisches Landesmuseum Karlsruhe. b. Harvard 1925.30.124, Hoppin bequest. Beazley, *Development* pl. 48.1. Photo, Fogg Art Museum, Harvard University.

57

ing the celebration of the first Great Panathenaia in 566 B.C. The eight
men named in it as *hieropoioi* say that they were "the first to accom-
plish the ἀγών for the girl with the owl eyes." We must keep much of
this evidence in mind as we consider the Parthenon frieze. We shall
approach it as a document of the festival. This is of course a limited
focus in considering such a work of art, but perhaps this method will
help in solving some much-debated problems. We must not expect,
however, that this representation, though full of life, is a portrayal
from life of the Panathenaic procession. It is a classical Ionic frieze,
rather, and therefore subject to strictly artistic conventions.

The theme of the Parthenon frieze is not the procession which took
place annually but the Great Panathenaia, the quadrennial festival,
for it shows the peplos, which seems to have been woven only every
fourth year.[7] Most scholars agree on this point but on many other
questions they do not. Brommer has discussed these different interpretations recently in his new publication of the frieze.[8] He rightly
rejects a mythological interpretation. The theme of the frieze is taken
not from myth but from cult, and it is necessary to stress this. It is
true that in certain representations the mythic and the cultic spheres
are mixed, for instance in vase-paintings with Herakles' initiation into
the Eleusinian mysteries (pl. 8). But because they show an etiological
myth one would never hesitate to count them also among cult pictures. The same reasoning may be applied in the case of the Parthenon frieze. If it showed the foundation of the Panathenaia by the
Athenian king, Kekrops, as some scholars believe,[9] it would be mythological, too. I follow Brommer in rejecting a mythological interpretation, but this aspect is irrelevant here because we speak about cult.

John Boardman has recently offered a more historical interpretation,[10] and this has to be considered. He argues that the horsemen

1949) Nos. 326–28. On the time of the foundation see Parke 33–34: "The Pythian
games at Delphi became a regular institution from 582 B.C. They were followed by the
Isthmian games from 581 and the Nemean games from 573. So Athens was very much
in a contemporary fashion in founding a recurrent series of contests." For Peisistratos
as founder of the Panathenaia see Shear (supra n. 28 to chapter 1) 3–4, 7–8.

7. Brommer, *PF* 145–46.

8. Brommer, *PF* 239–41, 246–47, 255–70.

9. Ch. Kardara, "Γλαυκῶπις—Ὁ Ἀρχαῖος Ναὸς καὶ τὸ θέμα τῆς ζωφόρου τοῦ
Παρθενῶνος," *ArchEph* 1961 (publ. 1964) 115–58; Ch. Jeppesen, "Bild und Mythus
an dem Parthenon," *ActaA* 34 (1963) 23–33.

10. J. Boardman, "The Parthenon Frieze—Another View," *Festschrift für Frank
Brommer* (Mainz, 1977) 39–49.

and the warriors in their chariots are a Panathenaic procession of heroes approaching the gods in the east frieze. These heroes are the Athenian soldiers who had been killed in the battle of Marathon. The twelve gods and the heroes of the ten Attic tribes are waiting to take these new heroes into their midst. The women at the head of the procession carry jugs and phialai for the libation with which the Marathonian dead will be greeted and accepted among the heroes. Though they had fought as foot soldiers, they appear, according to Boardman, with the genuine heroic attribute, the horse. He adds two surprising details. Six weeks before the battle of Marathon the Great Panathenaia had been celebrated by the same men who are shown in the frieze, and their number, if the drivers of the chariots are left out, is 192. The same number is recorded in Herodotus (6.117) for the Athenians killed at Marathon.

Boardman hoped to resolve questions concerning the frieze, but, as is often true of scholarly work, more new problems are raised than old ones solved. If these men are the Marathonian soldiers, why does Herakles, the main hero and god of that region, not greet them? And where are the other heroes of the battle who were shown in the painting in the Stoa Poikile, for instance Theseus?[11] Moreover, heroization does not mean total rejuvenation, as we know from many hero reliefs showing bearded men. The riders in the Parthenon frieze, however, nearly all seem to be of the same age. It is true that there is one older man, the bearded warrior in the center of the west frieze (pl. 21),[12] but he could be the military archon, the polemarch, as counterpart to the archon basileus in the center of the east frieze (pl. 20). The horsemen and charioteers were rightly called youths or, in Greek, *epheboi*. As we have seen in other Athenian festivals—e.g., the Mysteries (pl. 2.3) or the Plynteria—these young riders in military training were the normal escort of important processions in state festivals:[13] They accompanied the Holy Things from Eleusis, and the cult image of Athena Polias, as well as the peplos offered to this goddess at the Great Pan-

---

11. For the figures in this painting see T. Hölscher, *Griechische Historienbilder des 5. und 4. Jahrhunderts v. Chr.* (Würzburg, 1973) 50–68.

12. Brommer, *PF* pls. 23–24 (W VIII); there is only one other bearded horseman, figure 8 on W IV: Brommer, *PF* pls. 13–14. M. Robertson, *The Parthenon Frieze* (New York, 1975) 46, interprets these two bearded riders as the two *hipparchoi*, cf. Aristotle, *AP* 61.3; Lammert, s.v. "Hipparchos," *RE* 8.2 (1913) 1683, No. 20. But the hipparchoi were not involved in special cult functions, whereas the polemarch was, cf. Aristotle, *AP* 58.

13. See supra pp. 25, 48 and infra pp. 61, 82, 104.

athenaia. Thus I cannot see in these ephebes anything other than what they obviously are, and I think the traditional interpretation of them is right.

Boardman objects to the interpretation that the frieze shows a normal procession of the Great Panathenaia, because he misses "the girls who carry the hydriae and baskets . . . instead the hydriae are carried by men" (pl. 19.1).[14] But, as Jochen Schelp has shown in his monograph on the Greek offering basket, this implement is really represented in the right half of the east frieze, on the Louvre slab (pl. 22.1).[15] The girl at the head of the procession has given the basket to one of the marshals in front of her. She is the *kanephoros*, called after the kanoun, the basket for offerings. Among the three main shapes which were possible for the kanoun at that time, Schelp prefers to restore a basket with low rather than high handles. By its being placed in the hands of the Panathenaic marshal the impression is conveyed that the procession has just arrived at its goal, where the duty of the kanephoros ends and the offering begins.[16] Though the altar is not shown because of artistic convention, to the beholder in antiquity the action was clear: The girl is not about to receive the kanoun, or her arms would be extended; rather, she has just handed it over. Consequently, this scene is not set in the Agora, where some scholars would place it,[17] but on the Acropolis, near the altar. Before the victims were slaughtered, barley was taken from the kanoun and thrown over their heads. In the barley was hidden the knife with which the animals were killed.

14. Boardman (supra n. 10) 42. The youths carry the hydriai on their shoulders, and this was the Greek custom, whereas the girls carried them on their heads. Examples of male hydriaphoroi: Fikellura fragment from Miletos, P. Hommel, "Die Ausgrabung beim Athena-Tempel in Milet 1957. II. Der Abschnitt östlich des Athena-Tempels," *IstMitt* 9/10 (1959/60) 60.1 pl. 64.1; hydria London E 159, Beazley, *ARV²* 24.9: Phintias; skyphos Vienna Inv. 3710, Beazley, *ARV²* 380.171: Brygos Painter.

15. Schelp, *Kanoun* 55–56, pl.3.2; cf. Brommer, *PF* 122.

16. Schelp, *Kanoun* 19: "Die Tätigkeit der Kanephore endet am Ort des Opfers, d.h. am Altar. Dort übernimmt ein Opferdiener oder Priester den Opferkorb, wie Vasenbilder bezeugen und aus einer weiteren Aristophanesstelle hervorgeht" (*Peace* 948ff., 956).

17. Thus e.g., A. v. Premerstein, "Der Parthenonfries und die Werkstatt des panathenäischen Peplos," *ÖJh* 15 (1912) 1–35, and "Zur Deutung des Parthenonfrieses," *AthMitt* 38 (1913) 209–23; *contra:* Deubner 25, n. 6. It is true that the Twelve Gods and the Eponymous Heroes were worshipped in the Agora (Thompson/Wycherley 129–36, 38–41). But in the east frieze they are not worshipped themselves, but eleven of the Twelve Gods and the Eponymous Heroes are present to honor Athena; see infra p. 71.

It is not by chance that the kanephoros, who had one of the most prestigious functions in the whole procession, comes from the right side, that is from the side of the north frieze. Deubner and others have shown that this part of the procession, which overlooked the temple of Athena Polias and the precinct of Pandrosos, is the more sacred. In epigraphical records of the Panathenaia a clear distinction exists between the victims slaughtered in the "Old Temple"—later a part of the Erechtheion—and on the "Big Altar." Offerings within temples are an older rite than offerings on monumental open-air altars.[18] The meat of the former sacrifice was divided among priests and state officials, that of the latter was distributed to the populace. Whereas in the south frieze only cows are led to sacrifice, in the north frieze there are also sheep. These were offered not to Athena but to Pandrosos in accordance with an old Attic law, which prescribed a ewe for Pandrosos whenever Athena got a cow (Philochoros, *FGrHist* 328 F 10). It seems that Pandrosos did not have an altar of her own but rather had κοινοβωμία ("community of altar") with Athena. On a hydria in Uppsala (pl. 16.1) Athena's cow and the ewe of Pandrosos surround the altar of Athena within the Old Temple, indicated by a Doric column.[19] We must therefore imagine that the procession shown on the north frieze is proceeding to the Old Temple, whereas the procession on the south frieze is proceeding to the Big Altar. They came through the Propylaia together and then split into two lines. The cows and sheep in the north frieze are near the altar within the temple of Athena Polias, which was also the altar of Pandrosos.

To repeat: the north procession walks to Athena Polias, the ancient palace-goddess of the Bronze Age kings on the Acropolis, the south procession to Athena Parthenos, the goddess of democratic Athens. The first is more religious, the second more political and civic in character. But both are escorted by the same group of Athenian ephebes. Of course we must not suppose that the charioteers with their *apobatai* and the horsemen actually mounted up to the Acropolis. But they are included in the frieze to symbolize other parts of the procession and of the festival. The riders would escort the procession from its starting point at the Pompeion in the Kerameikos along the Pana-

18. For the phenomenon of altars within temples see Simon, *Götter* 77–78 with bibliography. North procession of the Parthenon more sacred: Deubner 25–26; Ziehen 470–74.

19. Melldahl/Flemberg 57–79, figs. 1–7, 12. We do not know an altar of Pandrosos in the Pandroseion; there stood the olive tree and the altar of Zeus Herkeios. The owl on the Uppsala hydria shows that this is Athena's altar.

thenaic Way to the foot of the Acropolis.[20] The chariots with their
apobatai represent the competitions (agones), which took place after
the procession day in the last days of Hekatombaion.[21] The chariots
and apobatai are deliberately chosen here because they symbolize a
time-honored contest and typical of Athens. On Late Geometric vases
apobatai are represented. According to H. A. Thompson there had
already been apobatic and other Panathenaic competitions in the Geometric Agora.[22]

Let us now look at individual groups in the two lines of the procession. In both lines a large group of men walks in front of the chariots
and the horsemen (pls. 18.3, 19.2).[23] For these bearded men the name
thallophoroi ("twig-carriers") is obstinately repeated by many scholars,[24] even though none of the men carries a twig and there are no
holes in their hands for metal attachments. Brommer thinks that the
olive twigs were painted, but painting leaves across the sculptured
folds of the garments would appear extremely clumsy. With fists empty,
however, is exactly the manner in which men in votive reliefs approach a deity.[25] The men, therefore, are not the most beautiful of the
elder Athenians, bearing olive twigs, but Athenian officials as we know
them from Aristotle (AP 60.1) and from Panathenaic inscriptions:
athlothetai, prytanes, hieropoioi, and so on.

In Carrey's drawing of the south frieze—most of the slab is lost—
four men with rectangular objects are walking in front of the ex-thallophoroi (pl. 18.3). In former publications they are called lyre players
because such musicians appear in the north frieze (pl. 18.2). But they
are dressed differently, and Brommer interprets their attributes as pinakes.[26] I think they are secretaries (γραμματεῖς), who are often mentioned in Panathenaic and other state inscriptions;[27] without registration,

20. For this way, the Dromos of Athens, see Travlos 422–28; Thompson/Wycherley
192–94 and passim.

21. Ziehen 474–86; for the apobatai see Brommer, PF 221–24.

22. H. A. Thompson, "The Panathenaic Festival," AA 1961, 224–31; Thompson/
Wycherley 121; on Geometric apobatai see also P. P. Kahane, "Ikonographische Un-
tersuchungen zur griechisch-geometrischen Kunst," AntK 16 (1973) 133 n. 80; Simon/
Hirmer 39.

23. Brommer, PF pls. 63–65 (N IX and N X), pls. 150–52 (S XXXV and S XXXVI).

24. See Brommer, PF 32–33, 217, with bibliography. But there are also critical
voices, e.g., Deubner 29; S. I. Rotroff, "The Parthenon Frieze and the Sacrifice to
Athena," AJA 81 (1977) 381; Parke 44: "It is perhaps unsafe to call them Thallophoroi."

25. For this ritual gesture see L. Deubner, "Götterzwang," Jdl 58 (1943) 91; H.
Prückner, Die lokrischen Tonreliefs (Mainz, 1968) 18, n. 110.

26. Brommer, PF pl. 113 (S XXXVII); interpretation as pinax-bearers ibid., 220.

27. See, e.g., Raubitschek (supra n. 6) No. 328. There are also statues of "scribes"

a fair distribution of meat to so many people was impossible. These secretaries are omitted from the north frieze because there the meat was divided only among the priests and state officials. In the south frieze the hieropoioi would dictate to them the number of victims, the order of distribution, etc., because the Athenian democracy was fond of accounts. The officials, formerly called thallophoroi, and the secretaries therefore belong close together.

In the north frieze musicians walk in front of the officials (pl. 18.2).[28] Animal offerings were nearly always accompanied by music. Thus two pipers and a lyre player are shown in an amusing procession in honor of Athena on a black-figured band-cup of the middle of the sixth century B.C. (pls. 16.2, 17.2).[29] In the north frieze there are four pipers and four lyre players. Deubner is surely wrong in stating that these belong to a lower class of the population; on the contrary, we know that members of a famous clan, the Euneidai, whose ancestor was the argonaut Jason, played the lyre at offerings in Athens.[30] They were of Lemnian origin and also held the priesthood of Dionysos Melpomenos. Euripides glorified this musical clan in his tragedy *Hypsipyle*. The north frieze is one of the earliest monuments to show them in their splendid robes, chiton with sleeves, peplos, and on their backs a mantle. Earlier *kitharodoi* wear only a chiton and a small mantle. The garment in the north frieze remains typical for these musicians throughout antiquity.

The youths with the hydriai in the north frieze (pl. 19.1) are a major problem because the sources—scholia and late lexika—speak of metic girls as *hydriaphoroi* in the Panathenaic procession. The scholarly explanation for this change of sex is a change of ritual,[31] for which we have no other evidence. Moreover, the metic girls with water jars mentioned tally with the other metic girls at the Panathenaia, who are attested by the same sources.[32] These girls carried chairs and parasols (διφροφόροι and σκιαφόροι) for daughters of noble Athenian citizens. I think the fact that the frieze represents the Great Panathenaia makes

---

among the archaic marble sculptures from the Acropolis; see B. S. Ridgway, *The Archaic Style in Greek Sculpture* (Princeton, 1977) 137, fig. 36, with bibliography.

28. Brommer, *PF* pls. 60–61 (N VII and N VIII); they were better preserved in Carrey's time: ibid., pl. 49.

29. Simon, *Götter* 193, fig. 176; E. G. Pemberton, "The Gods of the East Frieze of the Parthenon," *AJA* 80 (1976) 122, pl. 19.

30. Deubner 28; for the Euneidai see Toepffer, *AG* 181–206; G. W. Bond, *Euripides. Hypsipyle* (Oxford, 1963) 20; Maass, *Prohedrie* 125–26.

31. See Brommer, *PF* 217; for carrying hydriai on the shoulders see supra n. 14.

32. Hesychios s.v. "διφροφόροι" and schol. Aristoph. *Birds* 1550ff.; cf. Ziehen 465–66; Parke 44.

another explanation of the sex and number of the hydriaphoroi possible. They could be the victors in the annual torch-races, which took
place on the night before the Panathenaic procession.[33] There would
therefore be four of them at each Great Panathenaia. The inscription
of the early fourth century B.C. mentioned above tells us (line 77) that
the prize in that torch-race was a hydria. On a classical bell-krater in
the Fogg Art Museum a victor with his torch approaches an altar,
where his prize, a hydria, stands (pl. 22.2).[34] It has the shape of a
kalpis like the hydriai in the Parthenon frieze (pl. 19.1). The man in
priestly garb behind the altar is the archon basileus, who superintended all torch-races (Aristotle, AP 57.3). Perhaps it is no accident
that a late black-figure kalpis shows the well-known emblem of the
Panathenaic amphoras, a Palladion and columns (pl. 17.1).[35] We may
call this vessel a Panathenaic hydria, though the prize for the torch-
race was certainly of metal.[36] If this interpretation is correct, the four
hydriaphoroi connect the torch-races of the Lesser Panathenaia with
the great festival celebrated in the frieze. The victor of the previous
night, still exhausted, sets his vessel on the ground so that he can rest
a little.

The ritual significance of the torch-race was the transfer of sacred
fire for the offerings at the altar. For the Panathenaia the fire was
brought from the archaic altar of Eros in the Academy.[37] As we have
seen in the Arrephoria, connections between Athena and Aphrodite
are well documented in Attic religion, and excavations have shown
that Eros was venerated along with Aphrodite in the sanctuary on the
north slope.[38] Small wonder that he appears at his mother's side in the
east frieze.[39] Aphrodite points to the approaching procession; perhaps
the goddess has discovered the four young victors who had carried the
fire from the altar of her son to the altar of Athena.

Next in the north frieze (and in the south frieze immediately behind
the sacrificial victims) come youths with troughs on their left shoul-

33. Ziehen 459; Froning 78–81; Parke 45.
34. Harvard 60.344. CVA USA 6 Robinson Collection 2 pl. 47.2; Beazley, ARV²
1041.10: Manner of the Peleus Painter; Froning 80, n. 515; wrongly attributed to the
Kleophon Painter by me, "Ein nordattischer Pan," AntK 19 (1976) 20.
35. The hydria is in private possession in Florence.
36. For the shape see E. Diehl, Die Hydria (Mainz, 1964) 32.
37. Plutarch, Solon 1.7 and schol. Plato, Phaidros 231e; cf. A. Greifenhagen, Griechische Eroten (Berlin, 1957) 58, 60.
38. See supra n. 9 to chapter 3.
39. Brommer, PF pl. 179 (O VI). For the attribute of Eros, a sunshade, see ibid.,
263; the sarcophagus mentioned there is not in the Villa Giulia but in the Villa Albani.

ders, *skaphephoroi* (pl. 18.1).[40] According to late lexika they are young metics in purple gowns who carry elaborate metal troughs filled with honeycombs and cakes.[41] These implements may have been simpler in the fifth century. Honey was usually an offering in chthonic cults and its presence here will be explained below.

Let me emphasize what the south and north friezes have in common and what they do not. Besides the cows with their leaders and the officials (ex-thallophoroi) only the trough-bearers are present in both lines of the procession, whereas sheep, hydriaphoroi, pipers, and lyre players appear only in the more sacred north procession (pl. 18). Because the hydriai are shown to be heavy, they must be full and probably contain water.[42] Water and music were needed in the ritual slaughtering of the animals. Thus the nobler procession in the north frieze will be the first to sacrifice. The offering has just started, for the kanephoros who led this part of the procession has presented her kanoun to the marshal.

We have seen the number four many times in this procession of the north frieze. There are four cows, four ewes, four hydriaphoroi, four pipers, and four lyre players. This repetition has been connected by many scholars with the four ancient Ionic tribes of Attica.[43] It may be true that each of these tribes sent a victim, but the number of musicians is the same, and after the Kleisthenic reform the four old tribes were superseded by the ten Attic tribes whose eponymous heroes are represented in the east frieze.[44] The reiterated number four may not only hint at the Ionic tribes but may also be connected with the quadrennial cycle of the Great Panathenaia.

Susan Rotroff has recently come to a similar conclusion, namely that the foremost section of the frieze—that is from the east back to the officials in front of the chariots—does not represent simply the procession, but rather the sacrificial procession as it is regrouped on the Acropolis to proceed to the altar.[45] Hence it includes the victims and those essential to the sacrifice and omits the "διφροφόροι and σκια-φόροι [the chair- and parasol-carriers] who were not directly involved in the sacrifice." Scholars who have placed this part of the procession

---

40. Brommer, *PF* pls. 49, 57 (N V) and pls. 113, 152.2 (S XXXVII*). In the north frieze there are three of them; in the south frieze only one is preserved, ibid., 214.

41. Harpokration s.v. "σκαφηφόροι." Photios s.v. "σκαφας." Ziehen 466–67.

42. See Brommer, *PF* 30 with bibliography.

43. Deubner 27, n. 8; cf. Brommer, *PF* 215.

44. For them see Kron 202–14.

45. Rotroff (supra n. 24) 379–82.

in the Agora have felt the lack of the Panathenaic ship-car with the peplos as a sail. If the Acropolis is the scene, as Susan Rotroff has also argued, the ship is no longer a problem because it stopped at the foot of the Acropolis near the Areopagos (Pausanias 1.29.1). From there the peplos was carried, perhaps like a flag on the mast.

A still later phase in the transport of the peplos is shown in the central action of the east frieze (pl. 20).[46] A boy is helping a bearded man to fold it, a task for which two persons are needed because the cloth is big. Parallels with representations of priests on grave reliefs and vase-paintings show that the man wears priestly garb.[47] He has been correctly identified as the archon basileus by many scholars, including Boardman, who writes: "In a situation like this the obvious explanations must be the right ones."[48] The archon basileus will give the peplos to the priestess of Athena Polias, who at this moment is still occupied with two young girls. Some scholars have thought this peplos is the old peplos taken from the cult image before it was clothed with a new one. Athena, however, was disrobed on the *dies nefastus* of the Plynteria festival[49] and certainly not at the Panathenaia. The image need not have been clothed with the new peplos, which was instead added to Athena's treasures. The priestess may have put the folded peplos on the knees of the seated Athena Polias as the Trojan women did in the *Iliad* (6.303).

Boardman and Martin Robertson have proposed that the child who helps the archon may be a girl, one of the Arrephoroi.[50] Brommer, however, rightly argues that it is a boy, and he quotes a late antique source which speaks of a temple boy feeding the holy snake on the Acropolis.[51] There was also a statue of a boy described as a hockey player in the ball ground of the Arrephoroi.[52] The role of παῖδες ἀμφιθαλεῖς in Greek cults was so much taken for granted that sources about them are sparse; but in representations of offerings on vases a

46. Brommer, *PF* 263–70, pl. 174.1.

47. Parallels collected by Brommer, *PF* 268–69.

48. Boardman (supra n. 10) 41. The peplos was not destined for Athena Parthenos, as Parke maintains (33, 41), but for the cult image of Athena Polias.

49. See supra n. 25 to chapter 3.

50. Boardman (supra n. 10) 41; M. Robertson, *A History of Greek Art* (Cambridge, 1975) 308: "The small figure is always called a boy, perhaps rightly, but the strongly marked Venus-rings on the neck are surprising." Similar rings appear, for example, on the trough-bearer in the south frieze: Brommer, *PF* pl. 152.2.

51. Brommer, *PF* 269–70.

52. Deubner 15, n. 3; Parke (143) asks amusingly: "Was the ground used by boys as well as girls, or was there mixed hockey?"

boy usually helps in the sacrifice for a god or a goddess,[53] and the duties of a temple boy are beautifully described in the *Ion* of Euripides. On the east frieze the temple boy on the Acropolis must be represented. He was the ritual son of the archon basileus as the Arrephoroi were his ritual daughters.[54] The mythical predecessor of that boy was Erysichthon, the brother of Kekrops' three daughters, a young hero who had died early.[55] Whereas the Arrephoroi had been present at the Chalkeia when the weaving of the peplos began, the boy helps to fold it before it is presented to Athena.

Athena's priestess, a noblewoman of the Eteoboutadai,[56] is approached by two young girls with chairs (pl. 20). She helps the nearer and taller girl to take the chair from her head. The smaller girl has a smaller chair and carries in her left arm an object which is sometimes explained as a footstool; Dorothy Thompson and Boardman have seen little lion's paws as legs on it.[57] I think this is not a piece of furniture but something lighter, perhaps a small incense box. Thymiateria are carried by women in the east frieze,[58] and here would be the incense for them. In Roman reliefs with offering scenes incense boxes (*acerrae*) are often carried by young acolytes.

The two girls—children as is shown by their size—have been identified by scholars either as Arrephoroi or as *diphrophoroi*, the metic girls who carried chairs for the noble Athenian girls.[59] Those diphrophoroi, however, were minor characters, and it is unlikely that they appear in the main scene of the whole frieze. If we consider the ritual roles of the archon basileus and the priestess of Athena Polias as surrogates of the royal house it is probable that the girls are the Arrephoroi.[60] But why do the little successors of the Bronze Age princesses

---

53. See the examples collected by Metzger 107–18, pl. 47, and by Froning 52–57, pl. 15.

54. See supra nn. 6 and 16 to chapter 3.

55. The importance of Erysichthon for Attic cults is convincingly shown by Kron 93–94; see also infra n. 15 to chapter 5.

56. See supra n. 23 to chapter 2.

57. D. B. Thompson, "The Persian Spoils in Athens," in *The Aegean and the Near East. Studies Presented to Hetty Goldman*, ed. S. Weinberg (Locust Valley, N.Y., 1956) 290; Boardman (supra n. 10) 41. For the various interpretations of this object and of the two girls see Brommer, *PF* 266–67.

58. Brommer, *PF* 213. The incense box of the bride on the Ludovisi throne (Simon, *Götter* 248, fig. 238), though smaller (?), may be compared; also a fragment attributed to the Sisyphus Painter in a private collection in Basel: *RVAp* 1, pp. 16, 54, pl. 5.2.

59. See supra n. 32.

60. Deubner 12, 31 with bibliography.

perform the work of chair-carrying servants? Do they really provide the *diphroi* for the archon and the priestess as Boardman and others think?

A. Furtwängler interpreted these seats as ritual chairs for Athena's meal, holy things which could not be touched by everybody.[61] Investigations have shown that, like the Romans who celebrated *lectisternia* and *sellisternia* (in which beds and chairs were adorned and put up for gods and heroes),[62] the Greeks indeed knew ritual klinai, tables and chairs for *theoxenia*,[63] and *λεχεστρωτήρια as the name of a festival occurs already in Linear B.[64] In Greece this rite is especially attested in chthonic and hero cults.[65] In Athens and elsewhere klinai were put up for the Dioskouroi.[66] In the Deipnophoria, the festival of food-carrying for the daughters of Kekrops, sacred furniture was certainly used, and, because female guests did not lie on klinai but sat, these pieces of furniture were probably chairs.[67] In the Parthenon frieze the chairs carried by the Arrephoroi would thus seem to belong to female chthonic deities. But how does this fit with the Panathenaia?

Though Athena, sprung from the head of Zeus, seems to be the most Olympian of all gods, she has very strong chthonic connections. The statue of Athena Parthenos by Phidias was accompanied by a big snake, the chthonic being κατ' ἐξοχήν, and the Erechtheion, of which the temple of Athena Polias was a part, was mainly an edifice for chthonic rites, as Nikolaos Kontoleon has shown.[68] One of these was the cult of Pandrosos, to whom, as we have already seen, the sheep of the north frieze were offered. In all our sources on the ancient Acropolis there is no mention of a cult statue of Pandrosos, but in her

61. A. Furtwängler, *Meisterwerke der griechischen Plastik* (Leipzig and Berlin, 1893) 187–90; cf. supra n. 48 to chapter 3. Deubner (31 n. 14) wrongly rejected this interpretation.

62. G. Wissowa, s.v. "Lectisternium," *RE* 12.1 (1924) 1108–15; A. Klotz, s.v. "Sellisternium," *RE* 2 A 2 (1923) 1322. The latter was for the goddesses who sat on *sellae*, whereas the gods had *lectuli* (= klinai); tables were used for both.

63. F. Pfister, s.v. "Theoxenia," *RE* 5 A 2 (1934) 2256–58; K. Schauenburg, "Theoxenien auf einer schwarzfigurigen Olpe," *Mélanges Mansel* 1 (Ankara, 1974) 104–17; Kron 173.

64. Burkert, *HN* 237, n. 4; cf. also *Docs*[2]: 579, s.v. "re-ke-to-ro-te-ri-jo," (PY Fr 343, Fr 1217). Because klinai were not used in Bronze Age meals, this festival may have been a ἱερὸς γάμος.

65. See the "Totenmahlreliefs": Rh. N. Thönges-Stringaris, "Das griechische Totenmahl," *AthMitt* 80 (1965) 1–99; cf. also Simon, *Götter* 267–68, figs. 256–58.

66. See, e.g., Schauenburg (supra n. 63) pls. 57, 59b, 60a.

67. For the Deipnophoria see supra n. 50 to chapter 3; chairs used for female deities: supra n. 62.

68. Τὸ Ἐρέχθειον ὡς οἰκοδόμημα χθονίας λατρείας (Athens, 1949); Travlos 213–14.

precinct the olive tree and the altar of Zeus Herkeios existed, tokens of an ancient aniconic cult to which Pandrosos had belonged long before the etiological process made her one of Kekrops' daughters. For this reason a chair rather than an image may have been set up at the Panathenaia in order to give Pandrosos her part in the festival.

If this interpretation is correct, the second sacred chair must have served a similar purpose. There is indeed a second candidate. From the large inscription of the Salaminioi we know that Pandrosos and Kourotrophos had a common priestess who was a member of that Attic clan.[69] The altar of Ge Kourotrophos on the Acropolis was near or within the precinct of Pandrosos,[70] and was said to have been founded by Erichthonios. Ge Kourotrophos had borne him and was therefore honored in Athens as the nurse of children. Together with Athena Polias and Pandrosos she formed a triad in the offerings of Athenian officials.[71] Furthermore, a *prothyma* to Ge Kourotrophos was necessary at the beginning of every sacrifice in Athens;[72] the Panathenaic offering also must have begun with an offering to Ge Kourotrophos. She would have been invited to the sacrifice and therefore the second chair was for her. As she is more important than Pandrosos, hers must be the bigger chair, which is shown being put in place (pl. 20). As in the scene with the kanephoros and the marshal (pl. 22.1), the moment chosen for the representation is that immediately before the beginning of the sacrifice, which will start with an offering to Ge Kourotrophos. The two scenes in the east frieze are therefore synchronous.

In Homer beautiful women and children are the pride of a town or a region. Among the Homeric hymns, the thirtieth praises Ge, Mother of All, as the giver of beautiful children and crops and as the giver of sacred laws "in the town full of beautiful women" (11). In that splendid procession of girls and young women in the east frieze of the Parthenon, the Homeric ideal is present, together with gratitude to Ge Kourotrophos, who will receive the first offering.

We do not know what the prothyma for Ge at the Panathenaia was. Generally the barley from the kanoun, the holy basket, served as the first offering;[73] grain was a normal gift for chthonic deities. Yet there may have been something more for Ge Kourotrophos. As we have

69. Ferguson 21; M. Schmidt, "Die Entdeckung der Erichthonios," *AthMitt* 83 (1968) 208; Hadzisteliou Price 117.

70. Hadzisteliou Price 114, 117.

71. Deubner 27, n. 4; Hadzisteliou Price 114.

72. Suda s.v. "Κουροτρόφος." See Ferguson 21; Hadzisteliou Price 105–9, 111, 191–92.

73. See Schelp, *Kanoun* 93, s.v. "Voropfer."

noted, the troughs of the skaphephoroi contained cakes and honey-combs. Honey was a well-known propitiatory offering to chthonic gods,[74] and therefore I suggest that the honeycombs were offered to Ge at the Panathenaia. The cakes in the troughs may have been for Athena's chthonic companion, the snake, which was fed by the temple boy represented in the east frieze.[75]

Finally, the activity chosen for this frieze and the adjacent parts of the north and south friezes is not the offering itself but the very last preparations for it, and this tallies with the many cult scenes in Greek art. Thus most classical and Hellenistic votive reliefs show the worshippers arriving and the gods awaiting them. In the *Odyssey* Athena comes during the preparations of the sacrifice which Nestor gives in her honor (3.435–36): ἦλθε δ' Ἀθήνη ἱρῶν ἀντιάουσα. Homer does not say whether she is present visibly or invisibly.[76] In the east frieze it is clear that the gods are invisibly there, ἱρῶν ἀντιάοντες, and are waiting while the last preparations are made.[77] Athena still has her back turned to the peplos. The goddess's surprise at its beauty will be so much the greater at the moment it is presented to her. One may compare the scene on the New York oinochoe on which Pompe makes her final preparations behind the chair of Dionysos (pl. 5.2).[78] The god is curious and turns his head, whereas in the frieze Athena is waiting with dignity and Hephaistos tries to entertain her. The other gods relax (Dionysos), think about an absent person (Demeter), show impatience (Ares), or make conversation (Apollo and Poseidon); most of them behave informally because they feel unobserved. Of the gods only Hera is rendered with a formal gesture, but that is in character. The mortals are involved in their preparations; the heroes of the ten tribes, deliberately placed between gods and men, talk with each other.

74. P. Stengel, *Die griechischen Kultusaltertümer*[3] (Munich, 1920) 100–101; Kron (supra n. 25 to chapter 1) 145. There seems to be no monograph on the use of honey in Greek cults. Many honey-offerings are attested now in Linear B: cf. *Docs*[2]: 123, 131, 220–21, 223–24, 283, 308–10.

75. See supra n. 51.

76. The latter seems more probable because Homer does not say that they see her; they only pray to her.

77. For the representation of the gods in the east frieze see now the literature and discussion in Brommer, *PF* 257–58, and for the single gods, ibid., 258–63. Brommer follows Ph. Fehl, who places the gods on Mount Olympos: "The Rocks on the Parthenon Frieze," *JWarb* 24 (1961) 10–19 = *The Parthenon*, V. J. Bruno, ed., (New York, 1974) 313–21. One of Brommer's main arguments rests on the iconography of the east frieze of the Siphnian treasury. There the gods certainly are on Mount Olympos, because what is shown is a scene from the first book of the *Iliad* (Thetis and Zeus). This can by no means be compared with the theme of the east frieze of the Parthenon.

78. See supra n. 10 to Introduction.

It is not true, as some scholars have written, that these gods ignore men. They are waiting for them and some even look for the procession (Hermes, Iris, Artemis, and in front of all Aphrodite and Eros).

Boardman objects that in other offering scenes in Greek art not so many deities are present.[79] The east frieze tallies in this regard, however, with the east pediment and the east metopes of the Parthenon and last but not least with the peplos, on which, similarly, all Olympians were represented in the battle against the giants. The Gigantomachy may have been shown on the middle stripe of the peplos in a series of panels with the Olympians in single combat. An archaistic marble statue of Athena in Dresden has such an arrangement.[80] In any case, the Gigantomachy in the east metopes is a representation of what had been woven into the peplos which is being folded in the center of the east frieze. This is Athena's birthday present, whereas the east pediment showed the day of her birth.

Finally, there is no other temple where the three kinds of architectural sculpture—pediment, frieze, metopes—are so closely connected in their themes. In archaic art the Olympians were present at Athena's birth and in the Gigantomachy. In the east frieze they are also present at the celebration of her birthday. It is true that gods awaiting a sacrifice are new in Greek temple sculpture, but they are not at all new in Greek thought. Consider the first book of the *Odyssey*, where Poseidon has left Olympos to celebrate with his favorite people, the Ethiopians at the edge of the earth. Poseidon remains with them ἀντιόων . . . ἑκατόμβης (21–26). In the *Iliad* not only Poseidon but many other gods stay with the Ethiopians (23.205–8). In Pindar's dithyramb for the Athenians on the occasion of the Great Dionysia (F 75 Snell) the Olympian gods are invited to take part in the festival in honor of Dionysos. If the gods celebrate the City Dionysia, they can celebrate the Panathenaia, too. Thus not only the Athenians but also the gods honor Athena at her festival. At the same time they show their favor for Athens.

One might object that Greek sculpture was so selective that not everything that lived in Greek thought took shape in it. But Greek sculpture certainly represented the main themes of Greek life, and the communication between gods and men was such a theme. Indeed, in this respect the Parthenon frieze has forerunners in Greek relief sculpture, namely in the votive reliefs and more precisely in the post-

---

79. Boardman (supra n. 10) 43.
80. F. Vian, *Répertoire des gigantomachies figurées dans l'art grec et romain* (Paris, 1951) n. 44, pl. 14; E. Simon, *Pergamon und Hesiod* (Mainz, 1975) 41, n. 191.

archaic ones. On early reliefs either the deities or the worshippers were shown,[81] but from the fifth century on, deities and worshippers form part of the same composition. It is surely not by chance that one of the first examples of this type—still late archaic—was found on the Athenian Acropolis.[82] It shows a family offering a sow to Athena. As in the Parthenon frieze there is no altar; only the tall goddess, the family, and the victim are represented. The parallelism of this class of religious reliefs and the frieze around the cella of the Parthenon was surely deliberate. The Parthenon frieze is a votive relief, not of a single family but of the whole Athenian demos to Athena.

81. See G. Neumann, *Probleme des griechischen Weihreliefs* (Tübingen, 1979) passim; E. Simon, "Criteri per l'esegesi dei pinakes locresi," *Prospettiva* 10 (July 1977) 15–20.

82. H. Schrader, E. Langlotz and W.-H. Schuchhardt, *Die archaischen Bildwerke der Akropolis* (Frankfurt, 1939) pl. 175; Parke fig. 68; Ridgway (supra n. 27) 309, fig. 66.

5

FESTIVALS OF APOLLO AND ARTEMIS

Apollo and his sister Artemis had more influence on the names of Attic months than any other gods, and their festivals were deeply rooted in the Athenian calendar.[1] Nilsson considered the Greek months essentially post-Homeric and Parke agreed, dating none of the Athenian festivals of Apollo earlier than the eighth century B.C.[2] But many month-names occur on Linear B tablets.[3] It is true that the name Apollo has not yet been found in Mycenaean Greek,[4] and Burkert has convincingly shown that the Doric form Apellon comes from *apellai*, the assembly of the Doric people.[5] In spite of this there is evidence that Apollo's Athenian festivals, at least the older ones with which we are concerned here, must be dated back into the second millennium B.C.

In corroboration of his hypothesis of the Doric origin of Apollo's name Burkert writes: "The tradition of Athens seems to be quite directly rooted in the Mycenaean age; cults of Apollo on the other hand are peripheral in regard to placement and significance."[6] Burkert adduces as evidence two of the Athenian Apollo sanctuaries which he calls peripheral because they were situated outside the town, the Delphinion and the Pythion.[7] Both were near the Olympieion in a region which we already know to be the nucleus of very ancient Athenian cults. The Pythion with the statue of Apollo Pythios (Pausanias 1.19.1)

1. See supra n. 6 to Introduction.
2. Nilsson, *GGR* 644; Parke 149 and passim.
3. *Docs²*: 113–14, 278, 286, 303–5, 407, 475, 478–80.
4. For the problem of Apollo's name see *Docs²*: 126, 311–12, 476.
5. Burkert, "Apellai."
6. Ibid., 8 (my translation).
7. Travlos 83–90 (Delphinios); 291, fig. 379, No. 160 (Delphinion); 100–103 (Pythios); 291, fig. 379, No. 189 (Pythion?). Cf. O. Broneer, "Notes on Three Athenian Cult Places," *ArchEph* 1960, 54–62; Maass, *Prohedrie* 107–8; Wycherley 166–67 (Pythion).

is not yet identified with certainty, but recent excavations have revealed the Delphinion as an important early classical temple; according to legend its predecessor had been founded by Theseus. Because
the cult of Apollo Delphinios also existed in Miletos,[8] this legend cannot be pure fancy. In any case, the suburban situation of these two
sanctuaries can be explained by a time-honored function of Apollo,
ritual purification. Because this ceremony could not be performed inside a town, the Pythion and the Delphinion were located near the
Ilissos. Their peripheral location, therefore, was a necessity of cult
and cannot be used in Burkert's argument.

But Apollo had sanctuaries in the heart of Athens, too. In the temple founded by Peisistratos on the west side of the Agora he was called
Patroos, ancestor of the Ionians,[9] and as such he was venerated privately along with Zeus Herkeios in the house of every Athenian citizen (Aristotle, AP 55). The priests of Apollo had eight marble thrones
in the theater of Dionysos,[10] a number which is only matched by the
priests of Zeus. Last but not least Apollo was the possessor of a spec-
tacular cave on the northwest side of the Acropolis.[11] It was connected
with the birth of the eponymous hero of the Ionians, Ion, son of Apollo
and the Athenian princess Kreousa (Pausanias 1.28.4). The myth itself
may be later, but cult caves are common features of Minoan-Mycenaean religion, and the Acropolis cave was "the focus of Athenian Apollo
worship and the city's relation with Delphi."[12]

An important piece of evidence for the presence of Apollo in Bronze
Age Athens is the correspondence of his festivals and sanctuaries there
with those in Ionia. We have noted that Apollo Delphinios had a cult
in Athens and in Miletos; and the two oldest festivals of the god, Thargelia and Pyanopsia, were celebrated in Athens as well as in Ephesos,
Kolophon, and the rest of Ionia. The same would then be the case
with many common Ionic-Attic festivals for other gods, for example,
the Plynteria, the Apatouria, and the Anthesteria.[13] The alternatives

8. G. Kleiner, *Die Ruinen von Milet* (Berlin, 1968) 33–35. For Apollo in Athens and
in Ionia see infra p. 77.

9. Ferguson 29–33; Travlos 96–99; Maass, *Prohedrie* 128; Thompson/Wycherley
136–39; Wycherley 66–68.

10. Maass, *Prohedrie* 103–4, 107–8, 123–24, 128, 135–36, 138, 140.

11. Travlos 91–95.

12. A. W. Parsons, "Klepsydra and the Paved Court of the Pythion," *Hesperia* 12
(1943) 233–38.

13. For the Plynteria supra p. 46 and n. 25 to chapter 3; for the Anthesteria see
infra pp. 92ff. Apatouria as a common Ionian festival: Herodotos 1.147; cf. Deubner
232–34; Parke 88–92; cf. also Thompson/Wycherley 189–90. This was not a state festival but a celebration of the *phratriai*. Zeus Phratrios, Athena Phratria, and Hephaistos were honored.

for this correspondence are either that they entered Ionia when the Ionian colonization was funneled through Athens near the end of the second millennium (Herodotus 1.146) or, as Parke has suggested, they had come to Attica "from Asia via Delos in the eighth century or so."[14] It seems unlikely that so many cults were introduced into Athens from Ionia during the Late Geometric and Orientalizing periods, and even more improbable that they had been created by the Ionian colonists in Anatolia, because they are common to all Ionians. On the contrary, it is more plausible that these cults all have their origin in the Bronze Age. Thus the Apollo cults common to Attica and Ionia should be dated back to the time before the general migrations.

Finally, we must consider that Delos, the main sanctuary of the Ionian Apollo and the place of his birth, is connected with Bronze Age Athens in the following tradition: Erysichthon, Kekrops' son, was said to have brought from there the oldest Athenian image of the birth goddess, Eileithyia (Pausanias 1.18.5), a typical Minoan deity related to Artemis.[15] Erysichthon had his heroon in Prasiai near a temple of Apollo on the east coast of Attica (Pausanias 1.31.2).[16] Prasiai was the Bronze Age harbor of Athens for journeys to the Cyclades, whereas later on the Athenians would leave from the west coast, first from Phaleron and later from Piraeus. In the myth Theseus sailed to Crete from Phaleron. The myth of Erysichthon, who sailed to Delos from Prasiai, must go back to an earlier time when that eastern harbor was used for such travels.

Thus we see that Apollo did not come to Athens with the Doric migration but already belonged to the Minoan-Mycenaean pantheon. The myth of his birth in Delos corresponds to the Minoan conception of divine children.[17] At that time he did not necessarily have the name Apollo; he may have been called by one of his many later epithets, some of which, such as Phoibos, are really proper names.[18]

It seems to me that in Athens Apollo's precursor may also have been identical with the sun god Helios. Although we usually consider the identification of Apollo with the sun god as occurring relatively late, in the Hellenistic epoch, the Hellenistic mixture of Greek and foreign

14. Parke 148.

15. Hadzisteliou Price 150–52; for Erysichthon see supra n. 55 to chapter 4.

16. E. Meyer, s.v. "Prasiai" No. 2, *RE* 22.2 (1954) 1695–96. Sp. E. Iacovides, Περατή—Τὸ Νεκροταφεῖον A (Athens, 1969) 1–5.

17. The classic chapter on this conception is in M. P. Nilsson, "The Divine Child," in *The Minoan-Mycenaean Religion and Its Survival in Greek Religion* (Lund, 1950) 533–83; cf. Nilsson, *GGR* 315–24.

18. For instance *pa-ja-wo*, see *Docs*²: 311–12, 476; Burkert, "Apellai" 14–15; ibid., n. 56 for Phoibos; cf. also Burkert (n. 13 to chapter 1) 72–73.

religions sometimes revived very old traditions. We have seen, in connection with the festivals of Demeter, that among the Eteoboutadai there was a priest of Helios whose role seems to have been rooted in Bronze Age Athens.[19] And according to Philochoros, the most famous of the Atthidographers, Apollo-Helios and Ge were the progenitors of the Tritopatores, the ancestors of the earth-born Athenians.[20] Because the same belief in the sun god as the progenitor of a tribe existed in Italy, as Carl Koch has shown,[21] this origin may be a very ancient Indo-European notion. The sun god, together with the earth mother, was believed to be the source of Athens' autochthony. It is, therefore, not accidental that in some ancient authors the oldest Attic festivals of Apollo, the Thargelia and the Pyanopsia, are attributed not to him but to his Athenian forerunner Helios.

THARGELIA AND PYANOPSIA

These festivals, which gave their names to the corresponding months, had close interconnections and are therefore considered here together.[22] Both were celebrated on the seventh day of the month, Apollo's holy day and the day of his birth.

On 7 Thargelion and on 7 Pyanopsion, that is in May and in October, a procession went to the sanctuary of Apollo, probably the Pythion near the Ilissos or the Delphinion in the same region.[23] In both ceremonies the offering was a stew of different vegetables and grains boiled together in a pot (χύτρος): in May a stew of first fruits (θαργή-λια), in October of beans (πύανα) and other vegetables. The autumnal procession was also accompanied by a boy with two living parents (παῖς ἀμφιθαλής). He carried a branch of laurel, the Eiresione, which sometimes was decorated with various produce. It was fastened above the door of the sanctuary as a sign of fruitfulness, and the Athenians also seem to have put Eiresionai above the doors of their houses. In

19. See supra p. 24.
20. *FGrHist* 328 F 182; see Hadzisteliou Price 105. For the Tritopatores see E. Wüst, s.v. "Tritopatores," *RE* 7 A 1 (1939) 324–27; Travlos 302; Thompson/Wycherley 120, n. 19. The cult was typically Attic: instead of Apollo-Helios also Ouranos appears (cf. Wüst, ibid., 327), but Philochoros without doubt has the better tradition.
21. C. Koch, *Gestirnverehrung im alten Italien* (Frankfurt, 1933) passim; ibid., 113–18 about Philochoros.
22. Thargelia: Deubner 179–98; Bömer, "Pompa" 890–91; Parke 146–49. Pyanopsia: Deubner 198–201; Parke 75–76.
23. For the situation of these sanctuaries see supra n. 7.

the calendar-frieze a little boy with the Eiresione on his shoulder is walking in the month Pyanopsion (pls. 1.2, 3.1).

One would think that we are dealing with some ancient fertility rite like the Thesmophoria, were it not for the fact that ancient sources attribute these two festivals to Apollo or to Helios and the Horai.[24] In fact, the god of the Thargelia and the Pyanopsia was connected with vegetation. Apollo also had this function elsewhere: Apollo Amyklaios was the cult companion of Hyakinthos, a Minoan vegetation god,[25] and the Hyperborean gifts for Delian Apollo were hidden in stalks of wheat (Herodotus 4.33). The sources in which the god of the Thargelia is called Helios have been regarded by some scholars as late antique syncretism, but Deubner thought that in the processions at the Thargelia and Pyanopsia hymns may have been sung to Helios and the Horai, who were vegetation deities. I have already discussed (supra pp. 75f) the possible identity of the forerunner of Apollo with the sun god in Bronze Age Athens.

The more interesting festival is the Thargelia. It began on 6 Thargelion with the ritual purification of Athens. This was symbolically accomplished by expelling two men called *pharmakoi* ("scapegoats") after they had been fed at the expense of the polis. With the expulsion of the pharmakoi from the town all evil was believed to be eliminated from the populace and from the ripening crops. As was pointed out above, this ceremony is known from many Ionian cities, as far away as Abdera and Massalia.[26] The archaic poet Hipponax gives some details of the rite, for instance that the pharmakoi were beaten with the branches of wild fig trees.[27] They were even called *sybakchoi*, which seems to mean a number of figs gathered together, perhaps as counterpart to the bunches of myrtle, the bakchoi, borne in the Mysteries.[28] In Athens the Pharmakoi were given necklaces of dried figs to wear. As our sources explain, a necklace of dark figs worn by one phar-

24. Schol. Aristophanes, *Knights* 729 and other sources: see Deubner 191, n. 1; because Porphyrios (*de abst.* 2.7) also has this tradition, the common source may have been Theophrastos; see E. Pfuhl, *De Atheniensium pompis sacris* (Berlin, 1900) 87; Deubner 190–91; Jacoby's commentary on *FGrHist* 366 F 3.

25. M. J. Mellink, *Hyakinthos* (Utrecht, 1943): Nilsson, *GGR* 316–17, 530–35; Simon, *Götter* 121. For the Hyakinthia see J. Porter Nauert, "The Hagia Triada Sarcophagus. An Iconographical Study," *AntK* 8 (1965) 93–98.

26. For the Thargelia in Ionian cities see Nilsson, *GF* 105–15; V. Gebhardt, *Die Sybakchoi in Athen und die Pharmakoi in Ionien* (Munich, 1925); Deubner 181–88.

27. Hipponax F 5–10 in *Iambi et Elegi Graeci ante Alexandrum cantati*, ed. M. L. West (Oxford, 1971). For beating with fig branches see ibid., F 5.9. Also O. Götz, *Der Feigenbaum in der religiösen Kunst des Abendlandes* (Berlin, 1965) 140–43.

28. For them see supra p. 28.

makos and one of white figs worn by the other represented respec-
tively men and women.[29]

Figs must have been gathered for food in the Mediterranean region
long before grain was cultivated,[30] and therefore their meaning in cult
and magic was very complex. According to Attic tradition Demeter, a
deity primarily connected with food, showed the first fig to the ancestor of the Phytalidai, an old priestly clan (Pausanias 1.37.2).[31] In this
myth the fig is called holy (ἱερή), whereas at the Thargelia it seems to
be cursed. But like the Latin word *sacer*, ἱερός has both meanings.[32]
The necklace of figs worn by the kanephoros (Aristophanes, *Lysistrata*
646f.) was certainly holy, but figs at the Thargelia served as purificatory magic. The same can be said about the fig-bread which was carried in front of the Plynteria procession on the unlucky day in Thargelion
when the cult image of Athena left the city.[33] Purification for the purpose of securing the crops is a well-known practice in many cults.
Because he was a god of purification, Apollo was therefore also a god
of vegetation.

On the second day of the Thargelia the procession with the stew of
first fruits went from newly purified Athens to Apollo's sanctuary. There
were also contests of dithyrambic choruses of boys and men.[34] These
contests must have been a later addition to the old festival because
the eponymous archon—not the archon basileus—was responsible for
them, and the singers came from the ten Kleisthenic tribes (Aristotle,
AP 56.2). The victorious tribe set up a tripod in the Python near the
Ilissos. This scene is shown on a classical red-figure bell-krater in Copenhagen (pl. 23.2).[35] A hovering Nike is about to place a tripod on
the central column. The two fancifully dressed figures on the right are
singers of a dithyrambic chorus. The laurel tree and the skull of a billy
goat, a common offering to Apollo, place the scene in the Python. To
the left of the central altar a small acolyte presents a flat offering bas-

29. Hesychios s.v. "Φαρμακοί." Thus the man and the "woman" together represented the whole populace.
30. For the fig in Mycenaean times see *Docs*²: 608 s.v. "figs"; Richter (supra n. 20
to chapter 2) 142. For the fig in cult and magic: Olck, s.v. "Feige," *RE* 6.2 (1909) 2148–
50.
31. Toepffer, *AG* 247–54.
32. See, e.g., the wording ἱερὰ νόσος for epilepsy.
33. For this festival see supra n. 25 to chapter 3.
34. A. Pickard-Cambridge, *Dithyramb, Tragedy and Comedy*², rev. T. B. L. Webster (Oxford, 1962) 37; Froning 12, 17, 20.
35. Inv. Chr. VIII 939; *CVA* Denmark 4 Copenhagen 4 pl. 147; Froning 20, pl. 6.2.
For the tripods in the Python see Travlos 100.

ket to the priest. The sacrificial victim, in this case ordinarily a bull, is
not represented here.

A contemporary volute-krater from Spina in Ferrara shows Apollo
himself seated in his sanctuary (pl. 23.1).[36] The scene has been thought
to be Delphi, because the *omphalos* is present. But this chthonic symbol is found in many sanctuaries of the god, and the fact that there is
more than one tripod seems to fit better with the Pythion in Athens,
which was famous for its many tripods. In Delphi we would also expect to see the Pythia, whereas here a priest is waiting for the procession. A kanephoros with the offering basket still on her head approaches
the temple. Boys with bulls follow, painted in a style very similar to
the Parthenon frieze. I interpret this as an offering by the victorious
boys after a contest at the Thargelia. We may deduce that like Apollo
on this vase the cult image of Apollo Pythios in Athens was a seated
figure with a large laurel staff.[37]

Semni Karouzou has interpreted the representation on a small Late
Geometric cup in Athens as a dance at the Thargelia (figs. 9a–b).[38]
Men and women dancing are very common in Late Geometric art,
but the outside of this cup shows an uncommon motive, a frieze of
tripods (figs. 9a–b), which perhaps alludes to the Pythion. Apollo may
have been honored in Geometric Athens by dances of men and women,
which were later replaced by dithyrambic choruses. If this hypothesis
of Karouzou's is correct, we have here the earliest representation of
an Attic festival.

HIKETERIA (?)

On 6 Mounychion, the spring month named after Artemis Mounychia, a procession of girls walked to the Delphinion.[39] Each girl carried an olive twig bound with white wool, the ἱκετηρία ("suppliant's
twig"). The name of the festival could have been Hiketeria, which

36. Ferrara, T. 57 C VP. N. Alfieri and P. E. Arias, *Spina* (Munich, 1958) pls. 85–
87; Beazley, *ARV²* 1143.1: Kleophon Painter; Schelp, *Kanoun* 47; Parke
fig. 11.

37. A similar Apollo is shown on a bell-krater in Agrigento painted by the Kleophon
Painter, on which perhaps the Pythion in Athens is also represented: Froning 97, n.
130, pl. 16.

38. Athens, Nat. Mus. 874. S. Karouzou, *CVA* Grèce 2 Athènes 2 (1954) pls. 10–
11; Simon/Hirmer pl. 11; B. Borell, *Attisch-geometrische Schalen* (Mainz, 1978) No.
62, pp. 18, 65, pl. 14.

39. Deubner 201; Bömer, "Pompa" 1915; Parke 137. These authors do not give a
name to the festival.

Figures 9 a and b. Late Geometric cup, perhaps dance at the Thargelia. Athens Nat. Mus. 874; see p. 79. Photo, Deutsches Archäologisches Institut Athen.

would correspond to the ancient Roman *supplicatio*, a procession with suppliant's twigs and prayers for protection. Our only source for the Athenian festival is Plutarch in the life of Theseus (18.1); he connects it with the hero's departure for Crete. Initially the procession must have been performed as the result of a vow made in times of affliction and thereafter was maintained through the ages.

Because the sixth day of the month was holy to Artemis,[40] and because this was a procession of girls, this goddess surely took part in the festival. She was venerated along with Apollo in the Delphinion on the Ilissos, and the whole month Mounychion was sacred to her. The same was originally the case with the previous month, called Elaphebolion after the festival of Artemis Elaphebolos, the shooter of stags, although later the City Dionysia superseded all other celebrations. Artemis Elaphebolos is often represented in Attic art, for instance on a votive relief (pl. 24.1), but her festival, the Elaphebolia, had "dropped into unimportance."[41]

MOUNYCHIA

Artemis Mounychia is represented in the calendar-frieze beside the personification of Mounychion (pls. 1.1, 2.1). She wears a girdled peplos and a quiver on her back, and her right hand rests on the horns of a stag; in her left hand, destroyed by the Byzantine cross, she probably held a bow. She resembles the large fourth-century statue of bronze found in Piraeus,[42] which perhaps can be called Artemis Mounychia because the sanctuary of this goddess was on the peninsula there, which is still called Mounychia today.

On 16 Mounychion the festival Mounychia was celebrated for Artemis in Piraeus.[43] Artemis' holy day was normally the sixth, but the sixteenth was the time of the full moon, and Artemis Mounychia was originally more the moon goddess Hekate than the Olympian sister of Apollo. This is shown by the offerings which were brought to her in the festal procession: round cakes called *amphiphontes* ("shining on both sides"), which were also offered to Hekate at crossroads.[44] The ancient sources speak of δᾳδία ("little torches") which decorated them.

After the Persian wars the victory of Salamis was also celebrated on 16 Mounychion, although the sea battle had been fought seven months earlier in Boedromion. But because Artemis Mounychia had helped

40. It was celebrated as her birthday; cf. Diog. Laert. 2.44; Deubner 179, 201.

41. Deubner 209–10; Parke 125 (from there is the quote cited). The votive relief shown here in pl. 24.1 is in Cassel. M. Bieber, *Die antiken Skulpturen und Bronzen . . . in Cassel* (Marburg, 1915) 36, No. 74, pl. 32.

42. Athens, Nat. Mus., no number. Only preliminary publications of this important statue have yet appeared; for photographs see E. Vanderpool, "News Letter from Greece," *AJA* 64 (1960) 265–67, pl. 70, figs. 9–10.

43. Deubner 204–7; Parke 137–39.

44. Deubner and Parke, thinking of our birthday cakes, write of candles which had been stuck into the cakes. But candles, invented by the Etruscans, were used by them, not by the Greeks.

the Athenians against the Persian fleet, the commemoration was made a part of her festival. As in many state celebrations, the ephebes took part, this time not on horses but by ship. They performed a sea battle (*naumachia*) on ships which in some inscriptions are called sacred.[45]

Artemis Mounychia was also a goddess of the Athenian girls who served as "she-bears." Deubner's comments on this point are out of date because there is new archaeological material. I shall discuss this in connection with Artemis Brauronia (infra pp. 83–88).

CHARISTERIA

Like the victory at Salamis the victory at Marathon was not celebrated on the actual anniversary but some weeks after the battle at a festival of Artemis on 6 Boedromion.[46] The name of the festival, χαριστήρια, is recorded by Plutarch. Charisteria means "thanksgiving" and this is exactly what took place. According to Aristotle (*AP* 58.1) the polemarch, the military archon, performed the offering to Artemis Agrotera, the goddess of hunting and prey, and to Enyalios, the god of war, also known as Ares. Five hundred goats were slaughtered for them every year, a large number but much less than had been promised, because the Athenians had vowed to offer a goat for every Persian who fell in the battle. There were so many Persian dead that the Athenians could not find enough victims for Artemis and Enyalios. Indeed, as Parke writes, "the goat population of Attica would have been wrecked";[47] consequently, the number five hundred was set by the state. Escorted by ephebes in armor, the goats were led in a procession to the sanctuary of Artemis Agrotera on the Ilissos.[48] This sanctuary differed from the other Attic temples to Artemis because her companion was not Apollo, but Enyalios.

No picture of this procession with the many goats has yet been found, but we do have, I think, a representation of the month Boedromion with one of these goats on his lap. On the calyx-krater from Hermione in Athens is preserved a seated youth above whose head a sickle moon is shining.[49] He holds a white goat and is being crowned by a girl (pl.

45. Cf., e.g., *IG* II² 1011, line 16.
46. Deubner 209; Bömer, "Pompa" 1921 (instead of "Aigai" read "Agrai"); Parke 54–55. These authors do not give a name to the festival. Plutarch (*de Herod. mal.* 862a) calls it "χαριστήρια τῆς νίκης."
47. Parke 55.
48. According to Travlos (112–20), this was the so-called Ilissos Temple, but its identification is not certain, see supra p. 26.
49. See supra n. 9 to Introduction.

4.1). His companion also has a moon above his head but holds a laurel staff. This seems to be the Eiresione of the Pyanopsia, and the youth, therefore, is Pyanopsion who appears similar in the calendar-frieze (pls. 1.2, 3.1).

BRAURONIA AND ARKTEIA

The most famous of all Attic Artemis cults had its origin on the east coast of the peninsula at Brauron.[50] In the sixth century B.C. Peisistratos founded in Athens a Brauronion, a dependent sanctuary on the Acropolis where Artemis Epipyrgidia had been venerated since the Bronze Age.[51] After the Persian wars the influence of the cult spread to other Attic Artemis sanctuaries, but its center remained at Brauron, which flourished from the fifth century to Hellenistic times.

Our recent knowledge about the propagation of this cult comes from excavations and from the studies of Lilly Kahil.[52] In publishing the ceramic material from the Greek excavations at Brauron, she discovered a peculiar class of cult vessels which she calls krateriskoi (pl. 24.2). These are goblets in the shape of chalices with little rudimentary double handles, and a red-figure fragment shows that they seem to have been used for sprinkling water with twigs.[53] The krateriskoi are decorated with dark bands and some of them also have figures in the main frieze. These figures are little girls, naked or wearing short chitons, who hold torches or twigs and run or dance near an altar on which a fire burns; in many cases a palm tree is indicated at the altar. The style is cursory late black-figure, often without incision, or red-figure; the time is the period from the Persian wars to the end of the fifth century. These vessels were found all over the sanctuary and particularly in the region of the heroon of Iphigeneia, who, as we know from Euripides (*Iph.Taur.* 1464), was buried in Brauron. Recently Kahil has published fragments of three red-figure krateriskoi of the third quarter of the fifth century in a private collection; these show a much better style than the specimens hitherto known and therefore provide more details about the Brauronian cult.

One of the fragmentary vessels shows longhaired, naked girls run-

50. Deubner 207–8 is out of date; Parke 139–40 gives a short account of the new material.

51. Travlos 124–25; Artemis Epipyrgidia: Simon, *Götter* 158.

52. "Quelques Vases du Sanctuaire d'Artémis à Brauron," *AntK* Beiheft 1 (1963) 5–29; Kahil, "ArtémisAtt" 23–32; Kahil, "Brauron" 94–98.

53. Kahil, "ArtémisAtt" 24–25, pl. 8.8.

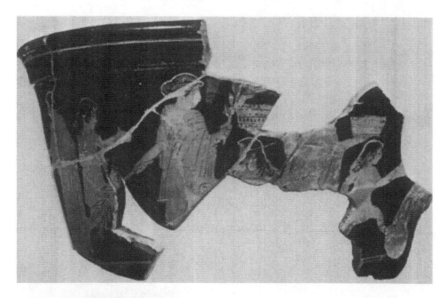

Figures 10 a and b. Brauronian arktoi on a krateriskos in private collection; see pp. 85, 86–87. Photo, D. Widmer, Basel.

Figure 11. Pyxis with personification of Delos (inscribed) and Leto, Apollo, Artemis, and Hermes. Ferrara 12451, from Spina; see p. 85. After drawing.

ning with crowns of leaves in their hands (fig. 10a);[54] most of them are young girls approaching their teens, but one is smaller. Near one handle two palm trees and parts of an animal are preserved (fig. 10b). This animal does not resemble the dogs hunting a fawn in the small frieze beneath the girls, and Kahil is surely correct in interpreting it as a bear, the animal sacred to Artemis Brauronia. Palm and bear are a strange combination because they come from different geographic regions, but they illustrate well how widespread the cult of Artemis was in time and space. The palm comes from Delos, the island of Apollo, where excavations have shown that Artemis had, in fact, been venerated earlier than her brother.[55] A pyxis of the last quarter of the fifth century from Spina shows the personification of Delos, identified by an inscription, sitting on an omphalos (fig. 11).[56] There is also a tripod and an olive tree and the triad Apollo-Artemis-Leto. The mother is standing near the holy palm tree under which she had borne her son, Apollo.

The bear, on the other hand, is a neolithic relic in the cult of Artemis. According to Karl Meuli, bears were the most important game for neolithic Eurasian hunting tribes.[57] The killing of these animals, which resemble man, was always followed by an expiatory rite like that of the Dipolieia to avoid the rage of Artemis.[58] From the Neolithic and from the Eurasian steppe the bear came to be the sacred animal

54. Kahil, "Brauron" 90–91, pl. 19; palm tree and bear: ibid., 91, fig. 4, pl. 19.2.

55. See, e.g., H. Gallet de Santerre, *Délos primitive et archaïque* (Paris 1958) 143–47.

56. Ferrara Inv. 12451. Beazley, *ARV²* 1277.22: Marlay Painter; G. Riccioni, "Delos e i Letoidi offerenti in una Pyxis di Spina," *Arte Antica e Moderna* 34/36 (1966) 173–81, pls. 70–72.

57. Meuli, *GesSch* 956 and passim. See also H. G. Buchholz, "Zum Bären in Syrien und Griechenland," *Acta Praehistorica et Archaeologica* 5/6 (1974/75) 175–85.

58. Simon, *Götter* 149–52; for the Dipolieia see supra n. 1 to chapter 1.

of the goddess; it was even dedicated to her in marble on the Acropolis.[59]

The etiological myths in Brauron and Mounychia tell of the wrath of Artemis because a she-bear had been killed in her sanctuary.[60] They also relate that the inhabitants, or the relatives of the killer, appeased the goddess with the following rite. Their unmarried daughters served in the sanctuary for a time during which they were called ἄρκτοι ("she-bears"), and the rite which they performed was called ἀρκτεῖα ("playing the she-bear"). This rite is shown on the krateriskoi: the little she-bears run or dance around the altar of Artemis. One of the recently published krateriskoi shows adult female marshals with twigs and baskets watching the little girls in short chitons (fig. 10a).[61]

These krateriskoi have been found in all Attic and Athenian sanctuaries of Artemis—in Halai, Mounychia, in the little temple of Artemis Aristoboule built by Themistokles, on the Acropolis,[62] and elsewhere. Kahil is surely right in suggesting that the *arkteia* was performed in all these places. The vessels are so numerous and frequently of such poor quality, however, that I cannot agree with Parke, who writes: "The practice of acting the she-bear was the duty and the privilege of a limited number of the aristocrats."[63] On the contrary, it seems that in the fifth century the whole populace took part in the arkteia and sent their young daughters, perhaps at the age of ten (some on the krateriskoi seem older, some younger) to the service of Artemis.

The cause of the sudden spread of this rite from Brauron all over Attica is undoubtedly to be found in the Persian wars, when Artemis was the main supporter of Athena's town and thereafter became one of the most important deities of the state.[64] We have seen that the victories of Salamis and Marathon were celebrated at her festivals. Perhaps in those troubled years the Athenians had vowed all their unmarried daughters to Artemis, but there is only the archaeological evidence, no literary source.

In what month or for how long the girls served in the different sanctuaries of Artemis we do not know. They certainly stayed overnight in isolated Brauron, in the classical Doric stoa which was excavated there.[65]

59. Kahil, "Brauron" pls. 21.6, 7. Deubner and others give as explanation for this attribute that Artemis herself once had appeared as a she-bear. The very reason for the preference for this animal, however, is given by Meuli (supra n. 57).

60. Deubner 205–7.

61. Kahil, "Brauron" 89–90, pl. 18.

62. The late archaic fragments from the Acropolis of Athens were shown by L. Kahil in a lecture in Philadelphia.

63. Parke 140.

64. Simon, *Götter* 175–78.

65. Christos Bouras calls this edifice "Parthenon" ("house of maidens" or "of the

Many marble votive statues of girls and also of little boys were found in the stoa; it therefore seems likely that Artemis Brauronia, as an extension of her role as goddess of the little she-bears, was also a Kourotrophos and perhaps a helper in childbirth.[66]

The third krateriskos published by Kahil introduces a final theme.[67] On one side we see Artemis, flanked by Leto and Apollo, shooting with bow and arrow, and on the other side, a seated male and a running female figure, each with a bear's head (pls. 25.1, 25.2). Because all other representations on the krateriskoi are part of the cult, Kahil also interprets this as a cult scene: a priestess and a young priest, perhaps of Apollo, with bear's-head masks. But I cannot agree that the running figure is also praying.[68] On the contrary, the gesture of the raised arms combined with running away expresses fright and consternation.[69] The bear's head, therefore, is not the mask of the Brauronian priestess (for which we have no evidence); rather, it signifies the metamorphosis into a bear. On a bell-krater in Boston, contemporary with the krateriskos, the transformation of Aktaion into a stag is indicated in a similar way by transformation of the head.[70]

If this interpretation is correct, we may go one step further. The arrow of Artemis is not directed against the little animal above the

maiden") from a Brauronian inscription in which a building of this name is mentioned: Chr. Bouras, Ἡ ἀναστήλωσις τῆς στοᾶς τῆς Βραυρῶνος (Athens, 1967); but others have shown that "Parthenon" was the name for the adyton of the temple of Artemis nearby. Kahil, "Brauron" 96–97, with bibliography.

66. Hadzisteliou Price 121–22.

67. Kahil, "Brauron" 92–98, figs. 6–8, fig. C, pl. 20.

68. It is true that the Bronze Age gesture of the raised arms, known from many Mycenaean idols, lingered in early archaic Greek art, disappeared afterwards, and turned up again in the later fifth century, the time of Kahil's fragments. The first figures, however, to show it again are archaistic idols, who stand stiffly and do not run. See Froning 58; E. Simon, "Aphrodite und Adonis, eine neuerworbene Pyxis in Würzburg," *AntK* 15 (1972) 23–24.

69. See G. Neumann, *Gesten und Gebärden in der griechischen Kunst* (Berlin, 1965) 97–105. Oreithyia and her companions are often shown with this gesture; see the vase-paintings collected by me in "Boreas und Oreithyia auf dem silbernen Rhyton in Triest," *Antike und Abendland* 13 (1967) figs. 8–11, 15. It is true that the head of these running figures is shown in profile, whereas the head and the upper body in Kahil's fragment are rendered *en face*. But the painter of the krateriskos wanted to show not only the consternation but also the metamorphosis of this figure.

70. Boston Inv. 00.346. Pickard-Cambridge, *DFA* 198, fig. 59. Beazley, *ARV²* 1045.7: Lykaon Painter; Kossatz-Deissmann (supra n. 15 to chapter 3) 147–48. This picture is closely connected with the *Toxotides* of Aischylos, a tragedy in which the metamorphosis of Aktaion was indicated by a mask; see Kossatz-Deissmann, ibid., 145. Aischylos also wrote a *Kallisto:* H. J. Mette, *Der verlorene Aischylos* (Berlin, 1963) 133–34; it seems likely that Aischylos also used the device of a mask to show the heroine's transformation on the stage.

handle but against the fleeing woman who becomes a bear and who
will be killed by the goddess. I think that this is the myth of Artemis
and Kallisto, mother of Arkas, a myth which Aischylos had brought to
the stage.[71] Arkas, the young sitting bear, is not threatened by the
goddess: as the ancestor of the Arcadians, he must survive; and Artemis, in spite of all her fierceness, was a Kourotrophos. But his mother,
who probably wears the bear's mask of the Aischylean tragedy, will be
killed and placed in heaven as the big she-bear.[72] The mythical theme,
it is true, is apparently an exception among the krateriskoi; but equally
exceptional is the quality of the vase itself.

71. See supra n. 70. For Kallisto in ancient art see A. D. Trendall, "Callisto in
Apulian Vase-Painting," *AntK* 20 (1977) 99–101, pl. 22.

72. Apollod. 3.101; see Mette (supra n. 70). There was also a statue of Kallisto on
the Acropolis (Pausanias 1.25.1) which may have been connected with the cult of Artemis Brauronia there.

6

FESTIVALS OF DIONYSOS

Finally I shall discuss the festivals of Dionysos, all of which occur in winter and early spring. Dionysos and Athens is an inexhaustible theme because to the Athenian cult of Dionysos belongs one of the greatest accomplishments of the Greeks, the tragedy. For this reason the festivals with dramatic performances, the Lenaia, the Rural Dionysia, and the City Dionysia are more thoroughly studied than any others. Our modern sources are not limited to the works of Deubner and Parke; there are also, among many others, the books of Sir Arthur Pickard-Cambridge.[1] Because the dramatic contests at the Lenaia and at both Dionysia are a relatively late development of the sixth century B.C.—the festivals themselves are older—I shall deal with them in the second part of this chapter, after we have considered two other Dionysiac festivals, the Oschophoria and the Anthesteria.

OSCHOPHORIA

This celebration took place on 7 Pyanopsion,[2] on the same day as the Pyanopsia, the festival of Apollo.[3] It is of great religious significance that these two diametrically opposed gods shared the same holy day, or rather that Apollo gave a part of his day, the seventh of the month, to Dionysos. Here we can see with certainty the influence of Delphi, because Apollo's oracle regulated and controlled the Dionysiac cults in Greece.[4] Moreover, the two gods also shared the sanctuary in Delphi: in summer Apollo was venerated there, in winter Dionysos. On a calyx-krater of the early fourth century B.C., now in

1. The most valuable of his "trilogy" (*Theatre of Dionysos; Dithyramb, Tragedy and Comedy*, and *DFA*) for our purpose is the last.
2. L. Ziehen, s.v. "Oschophoria," *RE* 18.2 (1942) 1537–43; Deubner 142–47; Ferguson 36–41; Parke 77–81.
3. See supra n. 22 to chapter 5.
4. Nilsson, *GGR* 573 and passim; Simon, *Götter* 292.

Leningrad, the young Apollo and the bearded Dionysos are shaking
hands in front of a palm tree near the Delphic omphalos (pl. 27).[5]
Apollo, we can tell, is leaving and Dionysos arriving, because the sat-
yrs and maenads of Dionysos' retinue fill the scene. One of them,
perhaps Thyia, the leader of the Delphic maenads, prepares a chair
for Dionysos. Because Apollo leaves Delphi in the fall and returns in
the spring, this picture must represent a Delphic ceremony which
corresponds to the time of the Pyanopsia. In the coming winter, in
Delphi as in Athens, the festivals of Dionysos will be celebrated.

In the calendar-frieze Dionysos is represented between the little
boy with the Eiresione (the laurel branch carried in the procession of
Apollo) and the woman with the kista of the Thesmophoria (pls. 1.2,
3.1).[6] He is beardless and naked and is pressing grapes with his feet.
In his right hand he probably held a thyrsos, which was only painted
on the frieze. The branch with grapes (ὦσχος) in his left hand indicates the Oschophoria. As Deubner has convincingly shown, this festival fell at the time of the vintage and wine-pressing and was therefore
a thanksgiving to Dionysos, the giver of the grapes.[7] Singing, characteristic of the whole celebration, was also part of the vintage itself, as
the Amasis Painter's amphora in Würzburg shows.[8] There a piping
satyr stands among his busy comrades.

The procession of the Oschophoria was headed by two *oschophoroi*,
youths with vine-branches full of grapes. The vine-branch was a well-
known attribute of Dionysos, especially on black-figure and early red-
figure vases, of which the most beautiful example is the Kleophrades
Painter's amphora in Munich (pl. 26).[9] As the large inscription of the
Salaminioi has revealed, the two young oschophoroi had to be noble
Salaminioi,[10] and we also know that they were clad as women. Deubner derived this from the Ionic chiton, the old dress of Dionysos shown

5. Leningrad St. 1807, from Kerch. Nilsson, *GGR* 614, pl. 38.2; H. Metzger, *Les
représentations dans la céramique attique du IVᵉ siècle* (Paris, 1951) pl. 37; Beazley,
*ARV*² 1185.7: Kadmos Painter.
6. The figure is not called Dionysos by Deubner (250), but the type is that of a
youthful Dionysos. Furthermore, there are no profane representations in the frieze.
7. The inscription of the Salaminioi was not yet known when Deubner wrote his
book. Ferguson, who published it, and Ziehen (supra n. 2) 1541–42, use the inscription to show that the Oschophoria were celebrated for Athena Skiras, although this is
nowhere said on the stone. L. Deubner, *Das attische Weinlesefest* (Abhandlungen
Akademie Berlin, 1944) 12, convincingly defends his interpretation of *Attische Feste*
142–47. For the inscription see also Sokolowski, *LS* Suppl. (1962) No. 19.
8. Martin von Wagner Museum L 265. Beazley, *ABV* 151.22; Simon/Hirmer pl. 68.
9. No. 2344. Beazley, *ARV*² 182.6; Simon/Hirmer pl. 121.
10. Ferguson 36; from other sources we know that both their parents had to be
alive: Ziehen (supra n. 2) 1538.

also on the Munich amphora. But these transvestites conform with other evidence for the mixture, known from many sources, of male and female features in the figure and the cult of Dionysos.[11]

The procession, led by the two oschophoroi, started from one of the Athenian sanctuaries of Dionysos—we do not know from which—and walked, singing, toward Phaleron, to the sanctuary of Athena Skiras, who was the patron goddess of the Salaminioi, members of an Attic clan which settled in Phaleron and Sounion.[12] Within the sanctuary of Athena Skiras was a precinct called the Oschophorion, where the offerings were made. Of the dances and songs performed there, some were cheerful, some sad (Plutarch, *Theseus* 22.4). Such a ritual was typical of festivals of vegetation deities, who were not immortal but died. Think of Attis, Adonis, Osiris, Hyakinthos, whose deaths were mourned in their festivals, or of the cult of the Charites founded by Minos on Paros.[13]

Parke, following Ferguson and some other scholars, considers the Oschophoria a festival of Athena Skiras. It is true that the Oschophorion was situated in her sanctuary, but we may compare this with the Pandroseion on the Acropolis, which was in the temenos of Athena Polias. The Salaminioi, who supplied the oschophoroi, also supplied the priestess of Pandrosos;[14] they seem to have specialized in vegetation cults. According to Parke, the concerns of Athena Skiras originally included the grape harvest.[15] This is puzzling because from early times and everywhere in Greece the god of grapes was Dionysos; the Salaminioi should not be an exception. We should expect instead that Athena took part in the Oschophoria as she took part in other vegetation rites performed for the well-being of her community, such as the Skira or the Arrephoria:[16] there she was connected with the growing of grain and with the olive. Why not also with the grape?

It is thus clear that the Oschophoria, although often omitted by modern scholars from the festivals of Dionysos, in fact touch on many

11. For this phenomenon see W. F. Otto, *Dionysos, Mythos und Kultus* (Frankfurt, 1933) 155–71.

12. See Ferguson passim; for Athena Skiras also supra n. 22 to chapter 2.

13. For the Charites see Kallimachos F 7 (Pfeiffer) with scholia and Simon, *Götter* 236. For the emotional side of the vegetation rites and the mixture of joy and mourning see generally Nilsson, *GGR* 324.

14. See supra n. 69 to chapter 4.

15. See Parke 80: "On transplantation to Attica it [that is, the Salaminian Oschophoria] was appropriately linked with the local cult of a wine-god by making the procession start from his shrine." Nilsson, *GGR* 586, n. 2, also thinks that the Oschophoria belong to Athena.

16. Supra pp. 22–24 and pp. 39–46.

of his most basic characteristics and may throw light upon other celebrations for him. Because of the vegetation aspect, this festival certainly goes back into Mycenaean times; and the name Dionysos is read
on two Linear B tablets from Pylos.[17] In Hellenistic and Roman times
the Dionysiac mysteries were celebrated at the time of the Oschophoria, which suggests that their more ancient and religious character
was recognized then.

ANTHESTERIA

This festival was celebrated for three days in the second week of
Anthesterion, from the eleventh to the thirteenth.[18] It was originally
the last of the winter Dionysiac celebrations and thus emerges as the
end of a Dionysiac cycle which began with the Oschophoria. The two
festivals may be regarded in some ways as two sides of the same coin:
the earlier one for the vintage, the later one for the first drinking of
the new wine after the pithoi were opened. Because the Oschophoria
were a vegetation rite, the Anthesteria must be one too, a fact apparent also from its name, the festival of flowers. Aside from this characteristic name, however, there is also evidence that the Anthesteria
were already being celebrated in the Late Bronze Age, the heyday of
vegetation cults. As we have already observed in connection with the
festivals of Apollo, celebrations common to Athens and the Ionian cities of Asia Minor should be regarded as belonging to the time before
the great migrations toward the end of the second millennium.[19] Thucydides and his scholiasts (2.15) argued that the Anthesteria must date
from a time before the dispersion of the Greek tribes during the Do-
rian invasion because they were celebrated by all Ionians. Burkert has
recently called them one of the oldest Greek festivals.

To Parke the Anthesteria seem to be a "curious mixture of ceremonies."[20] Burkert tries to connect them more closely with the phenomenon of bloody sacrifice by stressing—I think too heavily—the dark
side. If we view the Anthesteria mainly as a vegetation festival, the

17. *Docs*[2]: 127, 411. On the vegetation aspect of Dionysos: Nilsson, *GGR* 582–85.
Of course Dionysos was not a "primitive" vegetation god but connected with more
sophisticated agriculture. Farnell explained the trieteric festivals of the god convincingly with the "Zweifelder-Wirtschaft" (5:180–81); for this custom see Richter (supra
n. 20 to chapter 1) 100–101.
18. Deubner 93–123; Börner, "Pompa" 1936–37; Pickard-Cambridge, *DFA* 1–25;
Burkert, *HN* 236–69; Parke 107–20.
19. See supra pp. 74f., 77.
20. Parke 119.

combination of rites makes sense. Like the Oschophoria the Anthesteria also had a mournful aspect,[21] and one of the main ceremonies,
the sacred wedding (of Dionysos and the wife of the archon basileus)
was typical of vegetation festivals in the ancient Orient also.[22]

The central sanctuary of the Anthesteria was the Limnaion, the
temple of Dionysos ἐν λίμναις, that is, In the Marshes. Thucydides
mentions it along with the Olympieion and the Pythion (2.15.4); it
must therefore have been situated in the Ilissos region among its many
old sanctuaries; Pausanias does not describe it and it has not yet been
identified with certainty.[23] The temple was opened only at the. Anthesteria, whereas the temples of the other gods were closed during
this festival. Aristophanes makes his "Frogs" live near the Limnaion
and at the same time near the underworld, and we know from other
sources that the Anthesteria were also a festival of the dead and of
ghosts. They were thought to come to the meals in which free people
and slaves sat together, and at the end of the festival they were sent
away: "Off with you, ghosts, the Anthesteria are finished."[24]

The three days of the Anthesteria were called *Pithoigia*, *Choes*,
Chytroi. The first signifies the opening of the pithoi which contained
the new wine. Choes refers to the oinochoai or choes from which the
wine was poured into the drinking vessels; chytroi are the cooking
pots in which several kinds of grain were boiled together for Hermes
Chthonios (also called Psychopompos), who accompanied the dead.

Of what happened at the Pithoigia we do not know much. Surely
the arrival of the god, Dionysos, was celebrated. The famous procession with the ship-chariot, better known from the Smyrnaean Anthesteria, perhaps belonged to the first day and not to the second (or even
third) day, where Deubner has placed it.[25] The strange vehicle is rep-

21. For this phenomenon in vegetation rites see supra n. 13.

22. See Haussig (supra n. 20 to chapter 3) 53.

23. Judeich 176; G. T. W. Hooker, "The Topography of the *Frogs*," *JHS* 80 (1960)
112–17; Pickard-Cambridge, *DFA* 21–25; Wycherley 172, 195.

24. Burkert, *HN* 250–55, with bibliography.

25. L. Deubner, "Dionysos und die Anthesterien," *JdI* 42 (1927) 172–92; Deubner
102–11; Bömer, "Pompa" 1936–37; Pickard-Cambridge, *DFA* 12–13; Parke 109. The
latter authors follow Deubner in placing the procession with the ship-chariot in the
evening of the Choes, which, strictly speaking, belonged already to the Chytroi (see
supra n. 9 to chapter 2). Burkert, *HN* 223 with n. 26, on the other hand, connects the
ship-chariot with the Great Dionysia. This is not convincing because the god of that
festival, Dionysos Eleuthereus, did not come from overseas but from Boeotia (see infra
p. 103). Deubner and Nilsson (*GF* 267–71) were surely right in connecting the ship-
chariot with the Anthesteria. Because this procession, however, symbolized the arrival—the epiphany—of Dionysos (thus all scholars) it must have belonged to the first
day, the Pithoigia. The gods customarily were brought to their sanctuaries at the beginning of their festivals.

Figure 12. Ship-chariot on late archaic skyphos in Bologna; see p. 94. After Deubner pl. 11.1.

resented on black-figure Athenian vases (fig. 12).[26] It symbolizes the coming of Dionysos from the sea. Exekias' famous cup in Munich shows the same in a mythical picture.[27]

No other Athenian festival has left us so many vases as the second day of the Anthesteria. Wine jugs and drinking vessels could be bought in Athens at a market held specially for the festival. Such oinochoai are preserved in many sizes, from very small to very big, because everyone from three-year-old children to adults drank wine on that day. The prominent role of the children in this festival is due to its character as a vegetation cult. As we have seen in the festivals of Demeter and Aphrodite, childbirth and fertility were inseparable in the Greek mind. Dionysos himself was often represented as a child, for instance on Makron's cup from the Acropolis, on which Zeus carries the little Dionysos to the nymphs of Nysa.[28]

The illustrations in Deubner's book overflow with miniature jugs for

26. Deubner pl. 11.1 = Pickard-Cambridge, *DFA* 13, fig. 11; Deubner (p. 102) rightly criticizes this drawing; a photograph of the same skyphos in Bologna is in Parke, fig. 42. Other black-figure ship-chariots: Pickard-Cambridge, *DFA* figs. 12, 13; see also Princeton Symposium 74, n. 15 (M. I. Davies).

27. Simon/Hirmer pl. XXIV; Beazley, *ABV* 146.21.

28. Acr. 325. Beazley, *ARV²* 460.20. See also Simon/Hirmer pls. 190, XLVIII.

children, and of more recent work I mention only the studies by G. van Hoorn, J. R. Green, A. Lezzi-Hafter, J. Bazant, and E. M. Stern.[29] The last refutes Green's opinion that most of the little jugs had been made for child-burials. Of the thirty-eight graves of children found in the Kerameikos only four contained such miniature jugs. They were, therefore, mostly used in life and sometimes followed their little owners also into death. In other cases they were placed in the graves of children who had died before they reached the age of the Choes, because the parents thought they should have the joy of this festival in the underworld.

On many of the miniature jugs a jug (chous) of the same kind is shown, and vessels with such a representation may be certainly connected with the festival. Of course they were not the only presents given to children on this occasion; there were toys and pet animals, too. On a jug in Paris a child is approaching the altar of a boyish herm, behind which stands the little chous.[30]

We shall examine some jugs for adults, which were used for a drinking rite that also took place on the second day of the festival. As we know from the *Acharnians* of Aristophanes (1085ff.) and the scholia, the priest of Dionysos summoned distinguished persons to an official drinking contest in the building of the thesmothetai (somewhere in the southeast of the Agora).[31] Speaking was forbidden, and after a trumpet signal, drinking began in silence. The first to empty his chous was crowned as victor and given a full wineskin. Private contests, in which the prize was a cake, were also held on the same day. Usually at banquets everybody received his wine from the same mixing vessel, a large krater. But at the Choes, everybody brought his own wine already mixed in his oinochoe to pour in his own cup. A normal chous held twelve large drinking cups, that is, nearly three quarts.

On a large chous in Würzburg, Nike with a garlanded chous hovers in front of a young victor in such a contest (pls. 28.1, 28.2).[32] He walks

---

29. Deubner pls. 8, 9, 11, 13, 15–17; G. van Hoorn, *Choes and Anthesteria* (Leiden, 1951); Nilsson, *GGR* 587, n. 3; Metzger 58–64; Pickard-Cambridge, *DFA* 10–12, figs. 4–10; J. R. Green, "A Series of Added Red-Figure Choes," *AA* 1970, 475–87 and "Choes of the Later Fifth Century," *BSA* 66 (1971) 189–228; J. Bazant, "Iconography of Choes Reconsidered," *Listy Filologické* 98 (1975) 72–78; A. Lezzi-Hafter, *Der Schuwalow-Maler* (Mainz, 1976) 13–15; E. M. Stern, "Kinder-Kännchen zum Choenfest," *Castrum Peregrini* 132/133 (Amsterdam, 1978) 27–37.

30. Louvre CA 1683. Deubner 107, pls. 13.1, 2; Pickard-Cambridge, *DFA* fig. 3.

31. Thompson/Wycherley 125, n. 46; Wycherley 45.

32. H 4937. *Führer durch die Antikenabteilung des Martin-von-Wagner-Museums der Universität Würzburg* (Mainz, 1975) 141; Beazley, *ARV²* 871.95: Tarquinia Painter; F. Hölscher, *CVA* Deutschland 39 Würzburg 2 (1981) pl. 18.

with his little dog and his barbiton, carefully holding the last cup of wine for a libation to Dionysos in his sanctuary in the Marshes. The wineskin prize is not represented either because of artistic license or because this is only a victor in a private contest and he has already eaten his cake. In contrast to this graceful victor, on a chous in Athens we see Dionysos himself; he has definitely drunk too much.[33] A satyr supports him and a little satyr boy follows with a torch and the jug.

In considering the Attic festivals we have tried hitherto to differentiate myth from cult. But in Dionysiac festivals this distinction is often not possible because myth and cult in Dionysiac art usually form an inseparable entity, not only in dramatic performances but also in the visual arts. This is shown on many vases, for instance on a chous in Würzburg where a satyr is galloping on an ithyphallic mule, swinging his garlanded jug (pl. 28.3).[34] The picture is from the same period as the Parthenon frieze and parodies the Phidian horsemen.

The evening of the Choes, according to Athenian time-reckoning, belonged to the last day, the Chytroi, and was the time of the sacred wedding. Dionysos married the wife of the archon basileus, the so-called *basilinna* ("queen"). The ἱερὸς γάμος took place in the Boukoleion near the Agora, the official seat of the archon basileus (Aristotle, *AP* 3.5),[35] and was strictly secret. The wedding procession started from the Limnaion, where the basilinna had participated in sacred rites together with the fourteen *Gerarai*, Athenian women appointed by the archon basileus to make offerings at the fourteen altars in the sanctuary. The preparation for the wedding procession is symbolized on the New York chous with Dionysos and Pompe (pl. 5.2).[36] A high offering basket typical of wedding-processions stands between Pompe and Eros, who is fastening his sandal. Deubner's attempt to connect this picture with the ship-car procession is not convincing; I think we must differentiate between the arrival of the god from the sea on the first day of the Anthesteria and the wedding procession in the night following the Choes. These must have been two different *pompai*, one in which Dionysos arrived from overseas to take part in his festival[37] and one in which the basilinna was led to the Boukoleion.

33. Nat. Mus. 1218. Deubner pl. 8.3; Beazley, *ARV²* 1212.2: not far from the Shuvalov Painter; Lezzi-Hafter (supra n. 29) 14,92.

34. H 5387. *Führer* (supra n. 32) 140; R. Hampe, "Neuerwerbungen griechischer Vasen in Heidelberg und Würzburg," *Pantheon* 36 (1978) 112–13, figs. 15, 16; *CVA* Deutschland 39 (supra n. 32) pl. 16.

35. Other sources: Pickard-Cambridge, *DFA* 4–5; for the Boukoleion see Thompson/Wycherley 47.

36. See supra n. 10 to Introduction.

37. See supra n. 25.

The vase-paintings show that the bride of Dionysos was not accompanied by her bridegroom.[38] This is understandable because the mystery otherwise would have been profaned. On a privately owned skyphos a satyr clad in an ependytes walks before her holding two torches, symbols of marriage (pl. 30.1).[39] On a column-krater in Bologna, also from the middle of the fifth century,[40] the basilinna is led by Hermes, who took part in the celebrations of the Chytroi. Scholars have called the veiled bride Persephone, but the setting is not Eleusinian. There is an old woman with torches, one of the Gerarai, and a satyr carrying the dowry in a basket on his head. I think the scene shows the wedding procession setting out from the Limnaion.

After arriving in the archon's building the basilinna had to wait for her bridegroom. This is shown with a touch of humor on a calyx-krater in Tarquinia (pl. 31.1).[41] A satyr is sitting as the θυρωρός ("porter"), well known from wedding songs, on the threshold of the Boukoleion, inside which the bride sits on her bridal bed. That Dionysos is arriving from the drinking contest of the Choes is shown by his gait and by his companion, a small satyr holding a torch and the chous. A fragmentary calyx-krater in Tübingen shows Dionysos' bride sitting on the bed and being served by Eros.[42] Here also Dionysos is followed by a satyr with the typical chous, but the scene is very serious. Because the bride is identified by an inscription as Ariadne, the picture shows an etiological myth closely connected with the sacred wedding at the Anthesteria. In the myth Theseus had to surrender Ariadne to Dionysos. Accordingly, the archon basileus, the successor of Theseus, had to surrender his wife to the god. In the rite of the ἱερὸς γάμος the priest of Dionysos probably played the role of the divine bridegroom. At Thebes, Orchomenos, and Tiryns, the women of the Mycenaean royal

38. The common wedding processions on vases show the bride and bridegroom, often on a chariot, moving to their new home (see, e.g., Simon/Hirmer pls. XIII, 194). Vase-paintings in which the bride is alone (e.g., Deubner pl. 19 = Beazley, *ARV*² 1127.18: Washing Painter) need a special explanation. H. Goldman, "The Origin of the Greek Herm," *AJA* 46 (1942) 64ff. saw in some of them the basilinna. (The *loutrophoros*, ibid., 65, fig. 9 = Beazley, *ARV*² 1102.2: manner of the Naples Painter, is now in the Bad. Landesmuseum Karlsruhe.)

39. I have shown elsewhere that this type of vessel, the big skyphos, was also used at the Anthesteria: "Ein Anthesterien-Skyphos des Polygnotos," *AntK* 6 (1963) 6–22, pl. 2; Simon, *Götter* 279, fig. 269.

40. Inv. 236, from Bologna. *EAA* 1 (1958) 261, fig. 377; Beazley, *ARV*² 532.44: Alkimachos Painter.

41. RC 4197, from Tarquinia. Beazley, *ARV*² 1057.96: Group of Polygnotos; Simon (supra n. 39) 16, pl. 5.3.

42. Inv. 5439, from Taranto. Beazley, *ARV*² 1057.97: Group of Polygnotos. "Here too one thinks of the Basilinna" (Beazley); Simon (supra n. 39) 15–16, pl. 5.1.

houses went mad because the kings refused to embrace the cult of Dionysos; Agaue killed her own son in a maenadic frenzy. The Athenians, on the contrary, were wiser: Dionysos was accepted by them in the ritual of the sacred marriage.

A jug of medium size in New York shows a small bearded Dionysos sitting beneath a canopy of ivy together with children who, as Deubner suggested, are acting the sacred wedding of the god at the Anthesteria.[43] This proposal was refuted by Andreas Rumpf, and though his overly meticulous method is to be criticized, he is probably right here. The interpretation depends on the object which the three little boys on the left are carrying on their shoulders. Deubner thought it was the pennant of the ship-car of Dionysos. But on vases the ship-car is never shown with such an object, which looks more like a pole; indeed, on a bell-krater in Copenhagen (pl. 29) it seems to be a kind of Maypole.[44] That it is a portable object appears from the fact that it is set on a light base with three little feet. Half of the pole is covered with ivy leaves, which form the shape of an omphalos at its base. The association of this symbol of the earth-mother and the leaves shows that it is an artificial tree. In the cult of Attis, a vegetation god like Dionysos, there were *dendrophoroi* ("tree-bearers") and the name of one of the days of his festival means "the tree is brought in."[45] Therefore I should like to see in the two vase-paintings in New York and Copenhagen (pl. 29) the symbol of a tree carried in a Dionysiac procession. But we do not have literary sources for it.

On the Copenhagen krater this tree-like object is set down and a chorus of men accompanied by a flute player is singing around it. The singers are crowned with ivy; they wear ornamented robes; and some of them carry ivy twigs. They all have names—the piper is called Amphilochos, the man standing near the tree-symbol and shown with his bearded head *en face* has the well-known Athenian name Phrynichos, perhaps the comic poet of that time, and so on. Friis Johansen, who published this remarkable vase, saw here a dithyrambic chorus at the Anthesteria.[46] The official dithyrambic contests, however, were held

43. Met. Mus. 24.97.34. Deubner (supra n. 25) 177–79, figs. 7–9; Deubner 104–5, pls. 11.2–4; Rumpf (supra n. 12 to chapter 2) 210–12; Pickard-Cambridge, *DFA* 11, n. 8, fig. 10; Froning 27, n. 178. In spite of the strange drawing of the figures, the quality, e. g., of the ornament is remarkable.

44. Nat. Mus. 13817. K. Friis Johansen, *Eine Dithyrambos-Aufführung* (Copenhagen, 1959) 20, pls. 1–6; Beazley, *ARV²* 1145.35: Kleophon Painter; *CVA* Denmark 8 Copenhagen 8 (1963) pls. 347–49; Pickard-Cambridge, *DFA* 16–17, fig. 15; Froning 27–28.

45. M. P. Nilsson, *Geschichte der griechischen Religion* II (Munich, 1961) 644.

46. Friis Johansen (supra n. 44) passim.

at the City Dionysia, with which other scholars have associated the scene on the Copenhagen vase.[47] I would agree with this interpretation.

Two other rites of the last day of the Anthesteria have to be considered briefly. According to our sources, in the public rite of the Hydrophoria water was carried for the dead who had been killed in the Flood. Pausanias (1.18.7) describes a chasm near the Olympieion in the precinct of Ge, where the water of Deukalion's flood was said to have disappeared.[48] The legend of the Flood, a basic myth of the Middle East, was not very widespread in Greece, but it was alive in Delphi and Athens. It has been rightly supposed by Erika Diehl that a procession of girls with hydriai on their heads walked to the chasm, the drain for Deukalion's flood.[49] A number of late archaic hydriai with fountain scenes may be connected with this part of the Anthesteria.

The second rite, the Aiora ("swinging"), was more private. Boys and girls swinging are represented on classical choes, skyphoi, and hydriai, that is on vessels used during the three days of the festival. The most beautiful vase showing the Aiora is a skyphos in East Berlin (pl. 30.2).[50] The nymph Antheia—her name recalls the Anthesteria—is sitting on a swing and is being pushed by a satyr. Of course, swinging was also a children's game without ritual meaning. On a chous in Athens, however, the swing and the children are crowned for the festival (pl. 31.2).[51] According to Attic belief, the soul of Erigone, the daughter of Ikarios, was appeased by this ritual. Ikarios, who had introduced viticulture to Attica, was killed by his drunken fellow peasants because they thought he had poisoned them with the wine. Full of grief Erigone hanged herself from a tree. When the Athenians afterwards were struck by a plague the Delphic oracle advised them to hang up figures and masks in the trees and to put their children in swings in honor of Erigone. This magical purificatory practice is typical of the vegetation cult pervading the Anthesteria.

47. A. Greifenhagen, *Ein Satyrspiel des Aischylos?* (118 *BerlWinckProg* 1963) 5; M. Schmidt, "Dionysien," *AntK* 10 (1967) 80; Froning 27–28. I earlier (supra n. 39) 20, followed Friis Johansen, but I am now convinced that this chorus belongs to the Dionysia.

48. Travlos 290; cf. W. Borgeaud, "Le Déluge, Delphes, et les Anthestéries," *MusHelv* 4 (1947) 205–50.

49. Diehl (supra n. 36 to chapter 4) 130–34; but cf. also Jacoby's commentary on *FGrHist* 365 F4.

50. Inv. 2589, from Chiusi. F. Hauser, *FR* 3 (1932) 28–32, pl. 125; Deubner 118–20, pl. 18.1; Beazley, *ARV²* 1301.7: Penelope Painter; Simon (supra n. 39) 18–19, pl. 3.1; ibid., an interpretation of the other side.

51. Private collection, from Koropi. S. Karouzou, "Choes," *AJA* 50 (1946) 134, fig. 11; Beazley, *ARV²* 1249.14: Eretria Painter; Pickard-Cambridge, *DFA* fig. 9.

LENAIA

The festival for Dionysos Lenaios was celebrated in the middle of Gamelion, that is, towards the end of January.[52] The month Gamelion was called Lenaion in other regions of Greece, a month-name which occurs already in Hesiod (*Erga* 504). The main sanctuary of the Lenaia has not been identified with certainty, but there is some evidence that it may have been situated in the Agora near the Stoa Basileios.[53] According to Aristotle (*AP* 57.1) the archon basileus "superintends the Lenaean Dionysia, which consists of a procession and a musical contest. This procession he orders jointly with the superintendents (*epimeletai*) of the festival, but has sole charge of the contest." In the calendar-frieze a young Dionysos riding a goat, his holy animal, is shown in the month Gamelion (pl. 3.3).

The original Dionysos Lenaios, however, had a different appearance. In form he was a column with a bearded mask adorned with twigs. This idol was worshipped by maenads, who in the Ionic dialect could also be called *lenai*. The Lenaia, therefore, were the festival of the maenads. They must have formed the core of the procession mentioned in Aristotle. Many Athenian vases of the fifth century show the idol and the women.[54] The most famous are the cup in Berlin painted by Makron (pl. 32.2)[55] and the stamnos in Naples by the Dinos Painter.[56] On the latter a table with two stamnoi is placed in front of an idol clad in an ependytes.

Scholars from Nilsson to Burkert have tried to connect this idol with the Anthesteria,[57] but I follow Deubner, Parke, and many others, among them Beazley, who see here the Lenaia. There is, to be sure, a beautiful chous in Athens which shows the mask of Dionysos in a liknon and two women on either side holding attributes of Dionysos.[58] But

52. Deubner 123–34; Bömer, "Pompa" 1937; Pickard-Cambridge, *DFA* 25–42; Parke 104–6.

53. Judeich 293–96; Thompson/Wycherley 128–29; Wycherley 205, n. 7.

54. Pickard-Cambridge, *DFA* figs. 17–23. These vases were first collected by A. Frickenhaus, *Lenäenvasen* (72 *BerlWinckProg* 1912). His interpretation is still valid, although Nilsson, *GGR* 572, 587–88, connected these vase-paintings with the Anthesteria (Choes): see infra n. 58.

55. West Berlin F 2290. Beazley, *ARV*[2] 462.48: Makron; Simon/Hirmer pl. 169. (The Villa Giulia fragment has now been joined to the cup.)

56. Inv. 2419. Beazley, *ARV*[2] 1151.2–1152: Dinos Painter, "Feast of Dionysos (Lenaia)"; Simon/Hirmer pl. 212.

57. See supra n. 54; Burkert, *HN* 260–63, with the bibliography in n. 22; add Parke 106: "The best identification is that proposed originally by Frickenhaus and adopted by Deubner."

58. Private collection, from Anavysos. Nilsson, *GGR* 588, pl. 38.1; Beazley, *ARV*[2]

we have seen that not all representations on jugs of this shape are necessarily connected with the Anthesteria, and moreover, the wild dance of the maenads has no place in that festival of early spring. As we know from Plutarch, the Delphic maenads danced in the middle of winter,[59] and were joined every second year by a group of Attic maenads. Parke convincingly suggests that this group is represented on the Lenaia vases. Secondly, the interpretation that the column with the mask belonged to the Lenaia, not to the Anthesteria, is strengthened by the fact of the dramatic performances at this festival. Finally, Dionysos Eleuthereus, the idol of the City Dionysia, had the same shape as Dionysos Lenaios. As August Frickenhaus argued long ago, the form of this idol came from Thebes, where a log adorned with bronze was venerated as Dionysos Kadmos (Pausanias 9.12.4).[60] Eleutherai, the home of Dionysos Eleuthereus, is situated between Thebes and Athens.

RURAL DIONYSIA AND CITY DIONYSIA

Because the Rural Dionysia and the City Dionysia have been studied by so many scholars and because a full discussion would require too much time, I shall treat them only briefly.[61] Until the dramatic performances were added to the Dionysia in Peisistratid Athens, the City Dionysia were identical with those of the Attic countryside. Therefore I shall first consider the rural festival.

In the villages of Attica the Dionysia were celebrated in midwinter, in the second half of Poseideon. The festival fell within the second half of the month, but it was not celebrated simultaneously everywhere: the individual villages held it when they liked. The larger villages, for instance Thorikos, even had real theaters. In the calendar-frieze three men seated at a table heaped with crowns and other prizes (pl. 3.3) are the judges in the dramatic *agon*, and the two fighting cocks on the tablecloth symbolize that contest. Deubner calls the crowned woman beside the table Theoria, that is, the personification of beholding in

---

1249.13: Eretria Painter; Pickard-Cambridge, *DFA* fig. 24. This chous was used as an argument by Nilsson against Frickenhaus and Deubner (see supra n. 54).

59. Nilsson, *GGR* 570, 573; Parke 106.

60. See supra n. 54.

61. Pickard-Cambridge, *DFA* 42–101, has the best collection of sources and a thorough discussion. Cf. also Deubner 134–42; Bömer, "Pompa" 1937–40; Parke 100–103 (Rural or Country Dionysia), 125–35 (City Dionysia).

the theatron,[62] but I think she could also be Pompe, the personification of the procession at the Rural Dionysia. Aristophanes has dramatized this procession in his *Acharnians* (242ff.) and according to Aristotle (*Poetics* 1449a) comedy developed from it.

The main object in that procession was a large stylized wooden phallos which was carried and invoked; the parade was headed by a kanephoros and the victim was a billy goat. There is an Attic cup of the mid-sixth century B.C. in Florence on both sides of which a phallos procession is shown.[63] The kanephoros and the victim known from Aristophanes are not represented here. Tiny men carry the symbol on a tray. On one side a satyr ridden by a little man, on the other a large man (perhaps Phales, invoked in the songs), are associated with the phallos adorned with ivy and fillets.

The City Dionysia, the urban version of the rural celebrations, had the phallos procession, too. But this festival took place at another time, from 9 to 13 Elaphebolion, that is, in the second half of March. This date was chosen for purely practical reasons: the weather was warmer and people could watch the various outdoor performances more comfortably. The festival began with dithyrambic choruses of men and boys;[64] on the next day came the comedies; then followed three days of tragedies. On the calendar-frieze in the month Elaphebolion a comic actor with mask is leading a billy goat to sacrifice (pl. 2.1). *Tragodia* is etymologically connected with *tragos* ("billy goat"), but its exact meaning has been much debated by ancient and modern scholars.[65] In the frieze the tragos is certainly shown as a prize in the dramatic contest of the City Dionysia and as a typical victim for Dionysos. Victors in Dionysiac festivals used to offer their prizes—bulls or billy goats—to the god. The combination of the comic actor with the tragos symbolizes the two kinds of dramatic performances at the City Dionysia: comedies and tragedies. Whereas Aristotle had given both these dramatic genera different roots, according to the theory of the learned Hellenistic poet Eratosthenes, they had the same root.

62. Deubner 250–51; see supra n. 14 to Introduction.

63. Deubner 136, pl. 22.

64. On the bell-krater in Copenhagen (supra n. 44) a dithyrambic chorus at the City Dionysia is represented.

65. See Meuli, *GesSch* 255–58, 276–78; ibid., 256–258 about the Eratosthenic theory in the first century B.C. (Vergil). For Greek tragedy and sacrificial ritual see W. Burkert, "Greek Tragedy and Sacrificial Ritual," *GRBS* 7 (1966) 87–121; Burkert *HN* passim; also G. Else, *The Origin and Early Form of Greek Tragedy*, Martin Classical Lectures 20 (Cambridge, Mass., 1965): P. Pucci, "Euripides: the Monument and the Sacrifice," *Arethusa* 10 (1977) 165–95.

The calendar-frieze shows the Eratosthenic theory, which prevailed in the first century B.C.

The Dionysos for whom the city festival was celebrated had come from the countryside, from Eleutherai, the border fortress between Attica and Boeotia. A fragment of Euripides' *Antiope* (F 203 N), a tragedy which is set in Eleutherai, speaks of the form of the idol venerated there.[66] It was a στύλος, a column-shaped idol, as on the Kadmeia of Thebes. This was a typical Bronze Age shape—think of the column at the Lion Gate at Mycenae—to which a mask was added in archaic times. Many late archaic terracotta masks of the bearded Dionysos found in Boeotia testify to the popularity of this form (pl. 32.1).[67] On Attic vases which are contemporary with the foundation of the City Dionysia the mask of Dionysos appears often, and there is also the marble mask from Ikaria.[68]

These plastic masks cover only the face, whereas the masks worn by the actors covered the whole head. Though many Attic vases are inspired by the theater, scenes of actors performing with masks are very rare;[69] the vase painters preferred to show the myth instead of the play. But there is a half-chorus of actors wearing masks with diadems and short ornamented robes on a column-krater of the early fifth century B.C. in Basel (pl. 32.3).[70] Their arms are raised in a gesture well known from mourning men in funeral processions. They dance near an architectonic structure heaped with ribbons and twigs. This is not an altar, because there are no volutes crowning it; similar structures appear on some Attic white-ground lekythoi, where they are certainly gravestones. The object on the Basel krater is therefore a grave mon-

66. T. B. L. Webster, *The Tragedies of Euripides* (London, 1967) 205; B. Snell, *Szenen aus griechischen Dramen* (Berlin, 1971) 82, n. 19; E. Simon, *Das antike Theater* (Heidelberg, 1972) 9.

67. Heidelberg, Antikenmuseum der Universität TK 61. Simon, *Götter* 277, fig. 267; for the type see R. Hampe and H. Gropengiesser, *Aus der Sammlung des Archäologischen Institutes der Universität Heidelberg* (Berlin, Heidelberg, and New York, 1967) 100.

68. W. Wrede, "Der Maskengott," *AthMitt* 53 (1928) 66–95, pl. 1; ibid., 70–75, 90–91, other examples. For vases with the mask of Dionysos see Simon/Hirmer pl. XXVIII, with bibliography, p. 90.

69. They are shown handling masks before or after the performances, but not acting with masks on the stage. See the good collection of pictures in Pickard-Cambridge, *DFA* figs. 32–34, 49–55.

70. Antikenmuseum BS 415. Schmidt (supra n. 47) 70–81, pl. 19.1. Froning 23–24 shows that the chorus on this krater is not dithyrambic. It is certainly a dramatic chorus, but the figure on the left is not Dionysos Eleuthereus, as I previously wrote (Simon, *Götter* 273–74).

ument, and the twigs, ribbons, and mourning gestures fit this interpretation. The small figure half-hidden by this structure has been called
Dionysos, but this now is questionable. He certainly is not a column-
idol, because parts of his body beneath the himation are indicated.
And he wears a mask with open mouth. Karl Schefold has shown that
the whole situation implies a ghost who has been invoked by the chorus and emerges from his grave;[71] one might think of the ghost of
Darius in the *Persians* of Aischylos. The picture here, however, is
earlier and the figures are not dressed as Persians; their clothes and
their ankle rings suggest that they may be Thracians. The name of the
late archaic tragedy which they perform is not known.

   Though the Basel krater must be excluded from the representations
of the theater god, there is no doubt that the idol of Dionysos Eleuthereus had originally been a column with mask. His temple was a
Peisistratid foundation near the south slope of the Acropolis, and in
its neighborhood the theater developed. The City Dionysia began with
the arrival of the idol in its sanctuary. The idol had previously been
brought to the Academy and was now escorted from there in a procession to the temple at the south slope, with ephebes (as in other festivals) taking part in the parade. This was a ritual reiteration of the way
the god had taken at his very first arrival in Athens, for, whereas the
Dionysos of the Anthesteria had arrived with a ship from the sea, the
Dionysos of the Rural and City Dionysia was an inland god.

---

71. The interpretation given above was published by Karl Schefold, "Die Erschei-
nung des Toten auf einem Mischkrug des Basler Antikenmuseums," *Separatdruck
Schweizerische Kunst- und Antiquitätenmesse* (1974).

Conclusions

Viewed as a whole, Athenian festivals reveal themselves as remarkably conservative in spite of all historical changes in ancient Athens. At least three festivals have their roots in stone-age hunting and agricultural rituals: the Dipolieia, the Brauronia, and the Thesmophoria. The first preserved the most ancient offering rite for animals that we know of. It is true that the implements of the Dipolieia were remodelled in the Bronze Age by introducing a table and by substituting a bronze double ax for one of stone; but the practice itself remained unchanged. The rite of the she-bears at the Brauronia also preserved customs of the prehistoric hunting tribes. The Thesmophoria, on the other hand, reflected two great neolithic inventions, the cultivation of grain and its fertilization, tasks which were carried out by women. As did others of its kind, this exclusively female festival survived even after the Eleusinian Mysteries had been founded to honor the same goddess, Demeter.

From the Attic festivals of pre-Bronze Age origin—Dipolieia, Brauronia, Thesmophoria—we may conclude that the oldest cults of Attica were concerned with deities who were later known as Zeus, Artemis, and Demeter. What these deities were named in Neolithic and Early Helladic Attica we do not know. The word Zeus is Indo-European and came to Greece not earlier than the Middle Helladic period; but there may have been a chthonic god who was later called Zeus Meilichios, the god for whom the Diasia were celebrated. Zeus Polieus on the other hand, the god of the Dipolieia, was connected less with the soil than with human settlement. His female counterpart was Athena Polias. Most scholars maintain that she was venerated on the Acropolis earlier than Zeus, but this is questionable. In Rome, for instance, the cult of Iuppiter was earlier by far than the cult of Minerva in the Capitoline triad, and the rite of the Dipolieia came from the most remote past. As far as we can see, there is no festival of Athena in Athens which belonged to that oldest stratum of Attic religion, having its origins in or before the Neolithic period.

Typical Bronze Age festivals were the Eleusinian Mysteries, the Arrephoria, the older Panathenaia, the Lenaia, and the Anthesteria. In all of these the archon basileus played an important role as the successor of the Bronze Age kings, whereas he did not take part in the "neolithic" festivals considered above. We know Kekrops as the first of the Attic kings; the name may stand for a whole Middle Helladic dynasty. The struggle of Poseidon and Athena over the country is associated with Kekrops' reign. According to this myth, Athena came to Attica later than Poseidon, and this tallies with the fact that we know nothing about an Attic festival of neolithic origin for her. In the myth Athena calls Athens after herself (Hyginus *fab*. 164), but because she entered the Attic pantheon relatively late, she seems rather to have been named after Athens. The Athenian worship of the goddess must have been so exemplary and so well known that she was called "the Athenian" in other places.

If Athena was named after the town, Athens must have been important in Middle and Late Helladic times. This conclusion may explain the tradition that the Ionian migration toward the end of the second millennium was funneled through Athens and the fact that Athena was an important goddess in many of the Ionian towns in Asia Minor.

Another important goddess in Ionia was Artemis, who had been venerated in Attica earlier than Athena. With her and with Demeter, Athena—the new mistress of the country—had to accommodate herself. The procession of the Eteoboutadai at the Skira celebrated that arrangement every year. And the prehistoric forerunner of Artemis, Hekate, was honored as Epipyrgidia at the entrance to the Acropolis.

On the Acropolis itself there were two other goddesses older than Athena: Pandrosos and Kourotrophos. Pandrosos was connected with the olive tree which she, as her name indicates, nourished with dew. The name Kourotrophos is likewise connected with human offspring. In Athens this goddess was Ge, the mother earth, and by adopting the child Erichthonios from her Athena became a Kourotrophos herself. From Pandrosos, Athena adopted the olive tree, which was to become her most sacred Athenian attribute, the reason for her victory over Poseidon. With Ge Kourotrophos and Pandrosos, who shared the same priestess in historical times, Athena reconciled herself in a characteristic way; both of them shared in her main festival, the Panathenaia, and we have seen that the two chairs in the east frieze of the Parthenon are set up in their honor.

We do not know the place of origin of the goddess who was afterwards called "the Athenian" but her nature is clear. It is the type of palace goddess connected with the royal palaces in Bronze Age Greece and Crete as well as in the Near East. In oriental cultures this type of goddess is represented, for instance, by Ishtar, whose Hellenic descendants were both Aphrodite and Athena; perhaps this is the reason why Athena has a common festival with Aphrodite, the Arrephoria. This interrelation and the two little Arrephoroi, successors of the Bronze Age princesses, are specifically Attic.

In the Homeric poems, on the other hand, Athena is connected with Hera, whose cult was not prevalent in Athens. Hera's supremacy in Argos is reflected in the *Iliad,* where Athena often is not much more than Hera's messenger. In the *Odyssey* Athena acts independently, and it is perhaps not coincidental that the goddess, returning from Scheria, does not go to Olympos but via Marathon to Athens and into the house of Erechtheus (7.78ff.). Here she is surely depicted as "the Athenian."

As the palace goddess of the Athenian kings, Athena was also responsible for the well–being of the populace and therefore took part in vegetation rites, for instance in the Skira and the Arrephoria. On the other hand, we have seen reason to believe that the Oschophoria, attributed by many scholars to Athena Skiras, was, in fact, a festival of Dionysos. Because the two youths who led the Oschophoria procession had to be noble Salaminioi and because the Oschophorion, the goal of the procession, was situated within the precinct of Athena Skiras, it has been maintained that the festival was imported from Salamis to Athens in the sixth century B.C. But a useful parallel has been drawn with the Pandroseion on the Acropolis; for the priestess of Pandrosos and Kourotrophos had to be of Salaminian origin also, and the cult of these two goddesses was much older than the sixth century B.C., and was even earlier than the cult of Athena Polias. Furthermore, the Oschophoria, as the Attic vintage festival, belonged to the same vegetation cycle as the Anthesteria, and the antiquity of this festival is beyond doubt. Thus the Oschophoria and Anthesteria were twin festivals for Dionysos, both with roots in the Bronze Age: their connection with the figure of Theseus now becomes more meaningful.

Of the other feasts treated in these lectures the twin festivals of Apollo, Thargelia and Pyanopsia, seem also to be very ancient, although they cannot be defined with certainty as neolithic or as cults belonging to the palace culture. Because the archon basileus had no function in them, they are probably earlier than the time of the Bronze Age kings. Furthermore, the pulse, which was offered at both festivals, is known as an extremely ancient offering, older than the invention of bread-baking. Apollo, on the other hand, for whom in historic times the Thargelia and the Pyanopsia were celebrated, is explained by some modern authors as a relatively late intruder into Hellas, appearing not long before the time of Homer. They maintain that the two festivals in question had been celebrated originally for another deity unknown to us. The god of the Thargelia, however, was a god of purification, which was regarded as a basic requirement of fertility. And because purification was one of Apollo's main activities in historic times, his prehistoric forerunner must have been a similar god. He may not have been called Apollo, a name which is not yet attested in Linear B, but he may have been identical with the sun god. To Helios and the Horai, the vegetation goddesses, the Thargelia and the Pyanopsia are attributed in ancient sources, and this must be taken seriously. Furthermore, according to Philochoros, Apollo-Helios and Ge were the parents of the Tritopatores, the ancestors of the Athenians, whose cult was typical for Athens. And last but not least, among the Eteoboutadai there was a priest of Helios.

The ancient priestly clans of the Eteoboutadai, the Eumolpidai, the Kerykes, and others had important roles in Athenian state festivals, in spite of all democratic development. Aristocratic and democratic Athens come most beautifully together in the east frieze of the Parthenon. There the priestess from the noblest Athenian clan, the Eteoboutadai, and the archon basileus, the highest cult official of democratic Athens, carry out their roles side by side.

INDEX

The index is divided into the following sections: General index, Vase-painters, Ancient authors and sources, Modern authors.

GENERAL INDEX

Abdera, 77
Academy, 64, 104
Acropolis, 9, 15, 21, 26, 38, 40f., 48, 51f.,
    55, 60ff., 68, 72, 74, 83, 86, 91,
    94, 104ff.
Adonis, 91
aedicula, 48
Agaue, 98
Aghia Triada sarcophagus, 9, 77
Aglauros, 43, 45
Agora (of Athens), 26, 60, 62, 66, 74, 95f.,
    100
Agrai, 26f.
Aigeus, 44
Aiora, 99
Aktaion, 87
Alkamenes, 43, 53
Anaktoron, 34
Anatolia, 75, 92, 106
aniconic cult, 69
Ankyra, 48
Anodos, 18
Anthesteria, 74, 89, 92ff., 100f., 106f.
Anthesterion, 5f., 12, 92
Apatouria, 74
Apellon, 73
Aphrodisia, 48ff
Aphrodite, 40ff., 48ff., 64, 71, 94, 107
—in the Gardens, 40ff., 48, 51
—Ourania, 43f., 51
—Pandemos, 48ff.
apobatai, 61f.
Apollo, 4, 14, 28, 55, 70, 73ff., 81f., 85,
    87, 89f., 92, 107f.
—Amyklaios, 77
—Delios, 77
—Delphinios, 73f.
—Patroos, 8, 74
—Pythios, 73f., 79
Aquarius, 7
archaistic, 71, 87
archon basileus, 27, 29, 39f., 42f., 59,
    64, 66ff., 78, 93, 96f., 100, 106ff.
Areopagos, 66
Ares, 70, 82

Argos, 16, 50, 55, 107
Ariadne, 97
Aries, 7
Arkas, 88
Arkteia, 83ff.
arktoi, 42, 86ff.
Arrephoria, 38ff., 51, 64, 91, 106f.
Arrephoroi, 39ff., 46, 52, 66ff., 107
Artemis, 4, 16, 42, 48, 71, 73, 75, 81ff.,
    105f.
—Agrotera, 82f.
—Aristoboule, 86
—Brauronia, 83ff.
—Elaphebolos, 81
—Epipyrgidia, 83, 106
—Mounychia, 79, 81f.
Asia Minor. See Anatolia
Asklepieion, 48
Athena, 12, 22ff., 38ff., 50ff., 70, 78, 86,
    91, 106f.
—Ergane, 38f.
—Parthenos, 23, 68
—Phratria, 74
—Polias, 8, 12, 22ff., 40, 46f., 59ff., 66ff.,
    91, 105, 107
—Skiras, 22, 90f., 107
athlothetai, 62
Attis, 91, 98
autochthony, 76

bakchos, 28, 32, 36, 77
basilinna, 96f.
basket for offerings. See kanoun
bathing of cult images, 48f.
bear(s), 82, 85ff., 105
Bendis, Bendideia, 53f.
Big Altar of Athena Polias, 61
birthday, 55, 71, 76, 81
Boedromion, 5, 7, 24ff., 29, 81f.
Boeotia, 15, 18, 93, 103
Bona Dea, 17
Boukoleion, 96f.
Bouphonia, 8ff.
Boutadai. See Eteoboutadai
Bouzyges, Bouzygai, 21

111

VASE-PAINTERS

ANCIENT AUTHORS AND SOURCES

Aischylos
  Eumenides 13, 51
  —885ff. and 970ff., 50
  Kallisto, 87
  Persians, 104
  Toxotides, 87
Apollod., *Bibl*, 3.101, 88
Apollodoros of Athens F 113 (Jacoby), 50
Aristophanes
  Acharnians 242ff., 102
  —1085ff., with scholia, 95
  Birds 1550ff. with scholia, 63
  Clouds 408-9 and 864, 14f.
  —984 and 985 with scholia, 11f.
  Frogs 324ff. and 479 with scholia, 32
  —93
  Knights 729 with scholia, 77
  Lysistrata 641 and 646f., 42, 78
  Peace 948ff. and 956, 60
  Thesmophoriazousai 624 with scholia and 658, 18
  —834 with scholia, 20
Aristotle
  AP 3.5, 96
  —55, 8, 74
  —56.2, 78
  —57.1, 100
  —57, 27
  —57.3, 64
  —58.1, 82
  —58, 39
  —60.1, 62
  —61.3, 59
  Poetics 1449a, 102

Demosthenes, *c. Androt.* 13 with scholia, 47
Diogenes Laertios 2.44, 81

Eratosthenes, 102f.
Etymologicum Magnum, 55
Euripides
  Antiope F 203 (Nauck), 103
  Hypsipyle, 63
  Ion, 67
  Iph. Taur. 1464, 83

Harpocration, 65
Herodotus 1.105, 51
  —1.146, 75
  —1.147, 74
  —4.33, 77
  —6.117, 59
  —8.55, 46
  —8.94, 22
Hesiod
  Erga 391-92 and 393, 21
  —504, 100
Hesychius, 63, 78
Hippolytus, *Phil*. 5.8.39, 35
Hipponax F 5-10 (West), 77
Homer, Homeric, 19, 51f., 69
Homer
  Iliad 2.547-51, 51
  —3.277, 24
  —6.303, 66
  —23.205-8, 71
  Odyssey 1.7ff. (and 11.108ff.), 23
  —1.21-26, 71
  —3.435-36, 70
  —7.78ff., 107
  —17.297ff., 22
Homeric hymn to Demeter, 25, 29
  —202ff., 20
  —352, 32
  —441-69, 27
  —473-76, 29, 33
Homeric hymn to Ge 11, 69
Hyginus, *Fab*. 164, 106

Kallimachos F 7 (Pfeiffer), 91
Kallisthenes F 52 (Jacoby), 55

Lucian
  dial. mer. 2.1 with scholion, 19
  Icarom. 24, 15
Lykourgos F 48 (Blass), 52
Lysimachides F 1-9 (Jacoby), 23

Pausanias 1.1.4, 22
  —1.14.7, 44
  —1.18.5, 75
  —1.18.7, 99
  —1.19.1, 73

118

MODERN AUTHORS

WISCONSIN STUDIES IN CLASSICS

General Editors
Richard Daniel De Puma and Patricia A. Rosenmeyer

E. A. THOMPSON
Romans and Barbarians: The Decline of the Western Empire

JENNIFER TOLBERT ROBERTS
Accountability in Athenian Government

H. I. MARROU
A History of Education in Antiquity
Histoire de l'Education dans l'Antiquité, translated by GEORGE LAMB

ERIKA SIMON
Festivals of Attica: An Archaeological Commentary

PIERRE GRIMA
Roman Cities: Les villes romaines
translated and edited by G. Michael Woloch, together with A Descriptive
Catalogue of Roman Cities by G. Michael Woloch

EDITED BY WARREN G. MOON
Ancient Greek Art and Iconography

KATHERINE DOHAN MORROW
Greek Footwear and the Dating of Sculpture

JOHN KEVIN NEWMAN
The Classical Epic Tradition

EDITED BY JEANNY VORYS CANBY, EDITH PORADA,
BRUNILDE SISMONDO RIDGWAY, and TAMARA STECH
Ancient Anatolia: Aspects of Change and Cultural Development

ANN NORRIS MICHELINI
Euripides and the Tragic Tradition

EDITED BY WENDY J. RASCHKE
*The Archaeology of the Olympics: The Olympics and Other Festivals
in Antiquity*

BRUNILDE SISMONDO RIDGWAY
Hellenistic Sculpture III: The Styles of ca. 100–31 B.C.

ANGELIKI KOSMOPOULOU
The Iconography of Sculptured Statue Bases in the Archaic and Classical Periods